A
HOLY
RELATIONSHIP

A
HOLY
RELATIONSHIP

*The Memoir of
One Couple's Transformation*

JIMMIE LEWIS

SONOMA, CALIFORNIA

1+1=1 Publishing
1344 Jones Street
Sonoma, CA 95476

Email: 1plus1publishing@gmail.com

Copyright © 2014 Jimmie Lewis

All rights reserved. This book may not be reproduced in whole or in part, or transmitted in any form, without written permission from the publisher, except by a reviewer, who may quote brief passages in a review; nor may any part of this book be reproduced, stored in a retrieval system, or transmitted in any form or by any means electronic, mechanical, photocopying, recording, or other, without written permission of the publisher.

Publisher's Cataloging-in-Publication
Available on request

978-0-9914629-0-2 paperback
978-0-9914629-1-9 ebook

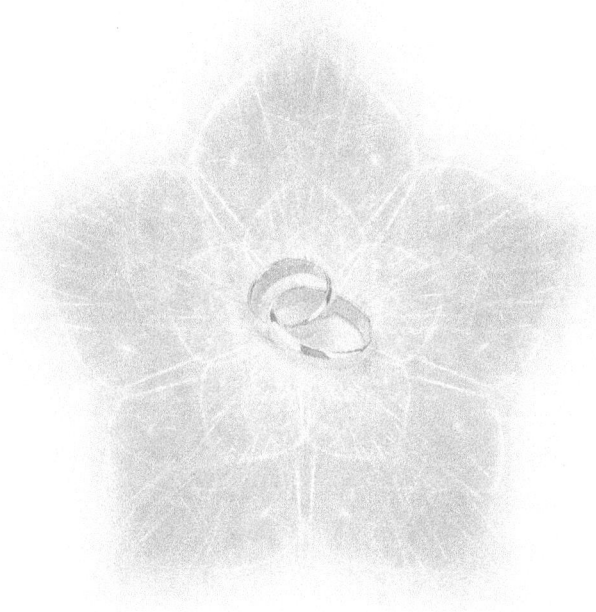

Dedication

This book is lovingly dedicated to my wife, partner, lover, playmate, pathmate, best friend and virtual co-author of this book:

BARBARA ANN KENNEY LEWIS
May 23, 1953 – August 31, 2010

Contents

	PROLOGUE	1
Chapter 1	A Secluded Beach	6
Chapter 2	Barbara's Early Life	21
Chapter 3	My Early Life	35
Chapter 4	Fear Creeps In	44
Chapter 5	Knowing and Being Known	54
Chapter 6	Into-Me-See	64
Chapter 7	The Two-Step Tango: Barbara's Version	68

Chapter 8	THE TWO-STEP TANGO: MY VERSION	79
Chapter 9	JUDGMENT: THE WORLD'S PRISON	85
Chapter 10	NON-JUDGMENT: GETTING OUT OF PRISON– BARBARA'S WAY	94
Chapter 11	NON-JUDGMENT: GETTING OUT OF PRISON– MY WAY	112
Chapter 12	SPECIAL RELATIONSHIPS	126
Chapter 13	1 + 1 = 1	137
Chapter 14	A TURNING POINT	152
Chapter 15	THE BEGINNING OF THE END	160
Chapter 16	THE GEWÜRZTRAMINER POPCICLE	178

Epilogue	194
Appendix	206
References	211
About the Author	214

Prologue

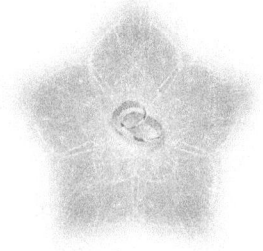

When you meet anyone, remember it is a holy encounter. As you see him you will see yourself.[1]

—A Course in Miracles

This book is virtually co-authored by my deceased wife, Barbara Lewis. That is because she is integrated within me and the me that is writing these words is the result of an extraordinary relationship that Barbara and I had over a 22 year period.

A Vehicle for Oneness

When Barbara and I finally met as single people, after years of knowing each other professionally, we knew instantly that our relationship was going to be "a vehicle for oneness", as we called it. We were both individually already on spiritual paths that were focused on awakening to the discovery of our true inner essence, which we each believed was the oneness of all creation.

The term, "holy relationship", was not something that was in our awareness at the time. It is a term that comes from the book, *A Course in Miracles*. I was already a student of the course but had no real appreciation of what a holy relationship was all about. Barbara became a student of the course right after we became a couple. Over time, as Barbara and I learned from, and practiced, the ideas from the course, we became keenly aware that the "vehicle for oneness" that we always wanted was our relationship *as* a "holy relationship" as described in *A Course in Miracles*.

One Unified Spirit

When two people see each other as one unified spirit they are in a holy relationship. How this is accomplished, and what this is about, is the gift of this book.

The title of this book is "A" Holy Relationship. It doesn't say "The" Holy Relationship or the "Only" Holy Relationship. There are many holy relationships out in the world. And there will be many more as time goes on. What I have written about is "one" holy relationship that I believe I have experienced. I needed to write about it so that I could further learn from it, so that I could fully integrate it, and to share it with the world for those of you that can learn from it.

Reflectation

I've also learned while writing this book, right near the end actually, that I don't have to rely on other people to have holy relationships because they start, and end, within my own mind, just as they start and end within yours. In what is probably best called "reflectation", lest you think I was in some type of formal meditation, I had a moment of communion with my deceased holy relationship partner, Barbara, and she said:

> *"Why limit yourself to only our holy relationship or only holy relationships where the other person sees you as one with her or him? Just because we had a holy relationship based on mutual knowing that we are one, that doesn't mean that you have to limit yourself to being dependent on the outside world in order to have holy relationships."*

I've explained in the epilogue that I don't actively commune with Barbara anymore and I've explained why. However, as I was finishing the epilogue and considering whether or not to have this prologue, I closed my eyes to reflect on the unlimited nature of holy relationships and those words of Barbara's came to me.

So I am now not limiting myself to holy relationships based on a two-way mutual intentional practice of transforming a special relationship into a holy relationship, which is what this book is about. However, this is the story of how Barbara and I finally got to what I believe was a holy relationship. Along the way, looking back on it, I know that we had countless moments that were holy in our relationship. Toward the end is where I believe we had a continuous holy relationship.

I don't think "our" way is the only way. In fact, as I point out in *A Holy Relationship*, *your* way is really the *only* way. And even without a partner, holy relationships are all around us, waiting for us to see someone else as ourselves. It is my sincerest prayer that there is at least one symbol of love in this book, represented by its words, that will resonate with you in such a way that your heart will open even more than it already is to the love that you are and that is all around you. And, from that love, you will extend yourself into countless holy relationships.

Metaphysics

I would also like to say that it has not been my purpose to try to explain my understanding of the metaphysics behind all of the ideas in this book. That is for another book and another book and another book.

However, I have used my understanding of metaphysics in those parts of the book where I thought it was necessary to fully explain something important relating to how Barbara and I created a holy relationship. For those of you whose spiritual path is different than mine, I hope you don't feel challenged by my version of the metaphysics behind the ideas in *A Holy Relationship*. I believe there is room within holy relationships for all paths and I hope that Barbara's and my experiences only bring you closer to your own holy relationships.

A Secluded Beach

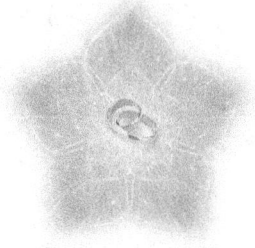

*The ark of peace
is entered two by two.*[2]
—A Course in Miracles

On a secluded beach in Hawaii in 1988 Barbara and I spent seven hours under the influence of the drug that I would later learn to be MDMA, but more commonly referred to as "ecstasy". Barbara had been introduced to MDMA by a male psychiatrist and female psychotherapist couple who were friends of hers and that later became my friends. Whereas most people, at least from what I've learned from most everyone I've ever asked about MDMA, use the drug as either a party drug and/or a wide-open-hearted huggy-feely connection with one or more people,

Barbara thought of MDMA as a relationship drug. She told me that by using it we would be able to "microwave" our relationship, meaning to open our hearts to such an extent that we could go much deeper, much quicker, into a much more intimate knowing of each other. We would be able to get to levels of intimacy that might take years, if ever, to reach.

I don't mean to endorse the use of illegal drugs here. But at the same time, I don't want to hide anything that contributed to this holy relationship. I see MDMA as I do anything else in physical form, as just another "form" that we've made up in this illusion of separation. The essence of all form is light, and all form will eventually return to its essence. I don't see any difference between MDMA and penicillin or a piece of toast. They are all agents of our mind that we use in this dream of an illusion. And how can anything that removes fear and opens us up to love be anything but wonderful?

My favorite lesson in *A Course in Miracles*, Lesson 135, addresses this issue. The lesson is entitled, "If I defend myself I am attacked". It says, "You operate from the belief you must protect yourself from what is happening because it must contain what threatens you ... And all [the world's] structures, all its thoughts and doubts, its penalties and heavy armaments, its legal definitions and its codes, its ethics and its leaders and its gods, all serve but to preserve its sense of threat. For no one walks the world in armature but must have terror striking at his heart."[3] So if Barbara and I broke a law that hurt no one, to facilitate the experience of removing fear and opening fully to love, I see no issue with it whatsoever. For those that do, I respect your point of view, but I have included the truth here because this whole book is about truth.

Love's Awakening

So with lots of water and sunscreen, and with music that we would forever associate with what we came to refer to as, "love's awakening", we openly delved into what would become the most important seven hours of our life. Then we spent the next twenty two years integrating into our relationship what we learned in those seven hours.

There was one thing Barbara wanted to disclose to me during that experience. It was the first of many, many … countless times … she would say, "I want to talk to you about something". I said, "Sure, what is it?" Her answer was, "I want you to know that I have breast implants." I instantly replied with, "Is that all? They're just vibrating energy. It means nothing." And with a big laugh and a huge sigh of relief she let go of that secret about herself that she was concerned might cause me to somehow dislike her or be disappointed in her.

It is my response about the vibrating energy that I believe the vision of Christ that we all have and are at our core, is all about. I didn't choose those words carefully or calculatingly. I didn't even think about what to say. I just blurted out a knowingness that came from deep within me, that everything is made, in its purest essence, of vibrating energy, the energy of life, the energy, or even purer, the light, of God. And why in the world would I ever want to judge the light of God? I gave that pure, unadulterated, unconditional love and acceptance to Barbara that day and in that moment, or holy instant, our holy relationship began to flourish. Please keep in mind that her courage to disclose began that holy instant that opened into the beginning of our holy relationship.

The vision of Christ. A holy instant. A holy relationship. What do those terms mean? Why am I using them? What are they about?

Well, they are just terms, or labels, of something deeper that is symbolically encapsulated in words that only represent something that cannot really be accurately expressed or explained. They can only be experienced. So please indulge me as I attempt to share with you my version of what I believe those terms represent.

The Vision of Christ

The word, "vision", is used to differentiate from the term, "sight". We have sight through our body's eyes. But what we see through our eyes are only perceptions, based on our inner beliefs of how the world works, that we project out onto the world and thus see what we believe. Vision is more like seeing truly, actually knowing, or experiencing, what something or someone is, instead of a perceptual representation of a person or thing.

The mechanism of sight is comprised of the thoughts and beliefs we make up in our minds that are based on our unconscious belief that we are separate from our source, whether you see that as God, Goddess, Higher Power, Allah, Jehovah, Yahweh, Buddha, Brahman or any other name including, perhaps, the more agnostic idea of the universe itself as our source. Our thoughts and beliefs, or perceptions, are based on the concepts we have about what we are and the world is. And we project our perceptions out onto the world and this is what we see. This is what sight is.

The mechanism of vision is the essence of who and what we really are. And what we really are is the extension of our Source into manifested creation, which is the light of creation that we are. All of us, in the aggregate, are that creation. And, as the individuals that we believe we are in human form, we are all really aspects of the one creation and are here to learn what we are not. We are not bodies. We are not individuals. We are not separate. We are one or, even better, One. A full realization of ourselves will one day be that we are all that is. We *are* the kingdom of God. We *are* the life God created. We *are* the very will of God. And what God creates can only be from, and of, Himself/Herself/Itself.

All that God is, we are, because God cannot be separated or divided in any way. Another way to look at it is that we are the thought or idea of God living in the mind of God. And, in that respect, *we* are the Christ. The one, collective *us* is the Christ. Jesus awakened to the Christ within and lived *as* Christ. We are all still awakening but will all one day live *as* Christ. So at our core, underneath the very bottom of the false belief that we are the separate self that we think we are, is God living within us and we can label that oneness with God as Christ.

Now can you imagine what the vision of Christ is? In that moment, in that holy instant, on that beach in Hawaii, the vision I had of Barbara's body was the essence of her body, vibrating energy or light atomically comprised into a physical body. And that physical body did eventually disintegrate and return back to the energy or light that comprised it. Barbara the spirit has never changed. She lives on beyond this dream of the physical plane.

The Holy Instant

In its purest form, as far as I can tell, the holy instant is any moment in which we are fully, totally, absolutely present in the essence of our being. I see it as a state of "presence" or living in the presence of being. By definition, there is no past or future in the holy instant. So if you are using your mind to "think" that you are in the holy instant, you are, by definition, "perceiving" that you are in the holy instant. And, if you are perceiving, that means you are using concepts, or beliefs, "about" the holy instant and so are not actually "in" the holy instant.

Being in the holy instant, from my experience, is the experience of being fully present in the moment, without any thought or belief, conscious or unconscious, about the past or future. You are totally surrendered to, and immersed in, what *is* right here, right now. You are experiencing, not thinking, and, in this state, you are living intuitively in a state of awareness of what you are experiencing.

In the holy instant, there is no resistance to what *is* right here, right now and there is no judgment about what *is* right here, right now. Rather, you are fully experiencing what *is* right here, right now. The feeling of that, the sense of that, is like an enlivened quickening throughout your body and a clarity of mind.

Imagine a sexual orgasm where you are totally surrendered and are fully experiencing what is happening right here, right now. Or imagine the beauty, the bliss, of a surrendered mother, allowing herself to live in the fullness of the moment, with only the freedom of surrender and the fullness of her breath as support, as she painlessly experiences the birth of her child. Or imagine letting go of a lifetime of worry and fear at the moment of death into the full experience of what *is* right here, right now. Or imagine the inspiration of a sunrise or sunset that draws you into the fullness of the moment, or the first moment a newborn baby is placed in the arms of the mother, and the fullness of those experiences right here, right now.

Once practiced, and delighted in, the holy instant can become a way of life in which we live intuitively in communion with spirit. That is the one spirit, created by God, that everything is and that we are.

A Holy Relationship

Two people sharing the vision of Christ, in a holy instant, are, I believe, in a holy relationship. To put it another way, less esoteric and more human and practical, when two people realize that they are not bodies, but one unified spirit, and are fully present in the moment, they have the conditions necessary to create a holy relationship. The only thing that needs to be added to the minds of both parties is the realization that neither of them, including themselves as a couple, is separate or different or special from each other or any other living being. It is the specialness that separates. It is the oneness that joins.

Creation is *one* thing. We are that creation. At the beginning of time, which is different from the instant of creation, the collective oneness of creation wondered what it would be like to be the source of our own power. It was like contemplating a power source and wondering how we could become that source. We imagined it for an instant and in that instant the terror and guilt of believing we had separated from God, from our Source, and therefore destroyed His creation, was so terrifying that we made up, in our collective one mind, the illusion of a physical universe to hide ourselves in, and split our one mind into countless aspects, each believing it knew best how to hide. We then made and hid in bodies and in various parts of the universe. And we polished it all off by repressing the whole thing never to be remembered so that we would never again feel that primal terror of separation nor the intense guilt for leaving our Creator. That is the dream, the illusion, we are living under.

A holy relationship begins when two or more people recognize their oneness at an intellectual level and consciously choose to live in experience of the moment with each other without judgment or any thought of specialness or separation.

When Barbara and I met in 1988 and knew we were going to be partners, we were each already on a non-religious spiritual path wanting only a personal and direct relationship with God. We knew immediately that our relationship was to be a vehicle for us to learn about our oneness with each other and, as such, as a vehicle for knowing our oneness with God and everyone and everything.

Marriage Vows

We wrote our own vows and were married by the beautiful and wise original founder of Unity Temple of New Orleans, Rev. Ruth Childress Murphy. She was then in her late eighties or nineties. To Barbara and me both, she absolutely glowed with love and kindness. Her body seemed to glow with the light of love, the divinity that animated her body. When we met her for a pre-marriage consultation she told us to "Stay in truth". Her last words to us after our wedding ceremony were to, "Stay in truth". That was on September 1, 1989. Her daughter, Rev. Ruth M. Elmer, is still there inspiring and leading people to "Stay in truth".

Barbara and I re-wrote our wedding vows in 1996 and re-dedicated ourselves to our vows every December 31st from then on. They were beautiful vows and we believed in them and did our best to live them. We eventually lived, and therefore transcended, them. We also replaced our original blue lapis and gold wedding rings, that we bought in Hawaii, with new gold and diamond rings because of the symbol of diamonds representing the idea of love living forever. In December of 2009, the last December of Barbara's life in the physical, we again re-wrote our vows and rededicated them on December 31 of that year. Barbara left the physical on August 31, 2010, the last day of our 20th year of marriage. The next day, September 1, 2010 would have been our 21st wedding anniversary. We were together 22 years, including our first year of living together.

First Re-Dedication of Marriage Vows

In the 1996 vows, there is a reference at the bottom of the ceremony to our guests that were there. There were no humans there, except Barbara and me. But we knew that Petrov, our main guide, Jesus our unofficial guide and mentor, God's Holy Spirit, and other "entities" from the non-physical plane were there. By 1996 we had had many, countless, experiences of communication with "entities" from what is commonly referred to as the "other side". These were through the crystal clear channel of communication that Barbara was. Our invitation was to them, to give them permission, and request, that they remind us of our vows any time they knew we might be straying from our path.

Here is a copy of those vows in the style in which we wrote them:

BARBARA ANN KENNEY LEWIS
JIMMIE CHARLES LEWIS
MARRIAGE CEREMONY: DECEMBER 31, 1996

Our intention:

*We are here before ourselves, and all of you,
to make a commitment to the oneness of our
relationship. We believe that only by becoming one
will we be able to plumb the depths of our own and
each other's Souls. We believe that by making a
commitment to oneness, we will reach the heights of
our natural state of happiness and joy. We believe
this is the most sacred and holy commitment that
two people on earth can make.*

Our wedding vows:

I believe that I have come on this earth to love you and to express how deeply the love of the Universe runs through me for you.

Therefore, I_____, hereby commit to becoming one with you, _____.

That means, I commit to changing all my thoughts, words and actions that see me as a separate entity and not one with you.

I commit to making our relationship my highest priority above all else, including myself.

I commit to fostering our spiritual growth together as a couple and, towards that end, I commit to openness and action.

I commit to honesty and to my own vulnerability and to create a space that fosters your vulnerability.

I commit to joining my dreams with your dreams, so that your dreams are my dreams, and all of my dreams are our dreams.

And, finally, I take responsibility for these vows and for the totality of our relationship.

Our rings:

I, _____, give you, _____ this ring as a symbol of my commitment to oneness with you, and in giving you diamonds, it symbolizes our oneness forever.

Our candle ceremony:

As we light our wedding candle from the two lighted candles, it symbolizes to us that we have now given up all rights to separateness. We maintain our individuality, but only in the context of our oneness. Our lights will shine not as separate individual flames, but as one holy, sacred and Divine flame.

Our invitation:

We now invite you all, our wedding guests, and give you permission to call to our minds, these vows of oneness if you see that we have strayed from our path of oneness.

Second Re-Dedication of Marriage Vows

Barbara and Jimmie/Recommitment Vows

We are One Mind, united with All. We see no separation between us and God and no separation or specialness between us and any living being.

Our purpose of being together is to reflect the qualities of the Son of God that we are, to each other and beyond to the world.

We give our relationship to the Holy Spirit for Him to use for His Holy purposes.

We commit to:

- Changing all thoughts of separation or specialness that might impede our experience of our Oneness.
- Giving our relationship and its purpose to the Holy Spirit that He might use it for His own Holy purposes.

We invite all of our guides, the Holy Spirit, Jesus, Petrov and God the Father to call to our mind any place we have strayed from these vows and our path of Oneness.

December 31, 2009

These vows are an encapsulation of what we believed was a holy relationship. I believe we embodied a holy relationship. This book is how we got there in hopes that you, too, will get there if you want to create a holy relationship, or holy relationships, in this lifetime.

Barbara's Early Life

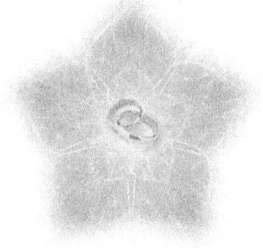

*The minute I heard my first love story
I started looking for you, not knowing
how blind that was. Lovers don't finally
meet somewhere. They're in each other
all along.*[4]

—RUMI

Barbara Ann Kenney came into this world on May 23rd, 1953. She chose a family that would shape and mold her in such a way that would eventually lead her to become aware within herself of two things that she saw as attributes of God: beauty and love. A third, unlimitedness, or unlimited abundance, she had to work much harder on to uncover within herself, but even this she did eventually learn to embrace within herself and express and enjoy out in the world.

Parental Conditioning

Barbara's mother came from a big family on a farm in Alabama and was raised during the depression years. She was tight-fisted and controlling and the ruler of the household. All of Barbara's clothes were either made by her mother or by Barbara herself.

Barbara's father was a loving, open-hearted man that allowed his wife to run the household and so kept the light of his love for his children smoldering in the large shadow cast by his wife. Nevertheless, Barbara became his friend and loved spending time with him on weekends as his helper of doing chores around the house. Barbara came away from this experience with both a deep love and affection for her father, and a feeling of being loved by him, and a thorough knowledge of how to be a handyman herself when it came to fixing and repairing things in her own, and eventually our, household. She was always the handyman and I was the helper.

Sibling Conditioning

Her middle brother was like her father, with a big open-heart and a love of people. However, he was easily influenced by the older brother and followed him along "like a puppy dog", according to Barbara. One year when it was time for the three children to get their shots for the next school year, Barbara's mother said she would give each of them a sucker (candy) if they didn't cry. Barbara's middle brother knew that she always cried and was terrified and, after he got his sucker, but before she went in to see the Doctor, he said, "Here, sissy. You can have my sucker because I know you will never get one from Mom."

Barbara repeated that story to me many times over the years and she carried that lesson of giving, when others couldn't give to themselves, with her all of her life. And she also carried an open-hearted love for her brother with her all the way to the grave, but never at the expense of her own hard-earned self-love.

Barbara's older brother was actually the virtual ruler of the household because he got away with abusing everyone in the family. Barbara's middle brother was consistently and continually physically, emotionally and mentally abused by the older brother. But when he was 17 years old, the middle brother had gotten bigger than the older brother and, right in the middle of a knock-down, drag-out fist fight the middle brother realized he didn't have to put up with the abuse anymore. In that moment, he flipped the older brother underneath him and ground his contact lens into his eyes (no real damage) and told him to never lay another hand on him again. And he didn't.

Transcending Abuse

What the older brother did to Barbara was different in nature but similar in severity. He convinced her that she was the "ugliest urchin on Earth" and that belief became a mainstay in Barbara's consciousness for years. He also hit her and beat her and even broke her nose one time as a child. The mother always discounted what happened when Barbara would run screaming and hollering to her that the older brother was about to kill her middle brother or some kid in the neighborhood and the same thing happened when he broke her nose. It was just written off like an accident and nothing was ever done to correct the little irregular crook in the middle of Barbara's nose.

The older brother would also accost Barbara in the hallway when she was a teenager when he was covered only with a towel and threatened to rape her. And he would throw her down on the floor in front of male friends of his, when they were doing drugs, and offer for them to rape her. The physical rape never happened but the mental and emotional scars remained for years.

You can see that Barbara, as we all did, had her own set of challenges as a child and that she left childhood with many issues that needed to be resolved before she could discover the love and beauty within herself.

At about age 35 Barbara polished off her inner psychological healing that related to her older brother's abuse with some intensive one-on-one and group therapy.

Barbara was always a fast learner, and did everything fast. So she was the very first member of her abuse group to leave the therapy and quickly invited her older brother over for a visit.

With me upstairs ready to run down to intervene if necessary, and our Weimaraner dog, Max, right by Barbara's side, she confronted her older brother and recounted the essence of everything he ever did to her. She took back her power in full that day and dismissed him from her life until she got to the other side of forgiveness. And as a symbol of her unwillingness to ever again receive what he was giving, which she knew was actually taking, she gave him back the cheap plastic umbrella that he had given her for Christmas. In that moment, Barbara's full power was unleashed and never left.

From Ugliest Urchin to Beauty Queen and Model

Barbara took care of the "ugliest urchin on Earth" false belief about herself as soon as she became a teenager and realized that she just might not be the ugliest urchin on Earth. She entered three beauty contests. She was runner-up in one. She won one. And she was one of the finalists for Miss Teenage America in a contest in Dallas.

After the formalities of the contest in Dallas were over, Eileen Ford, of the Eileen Ford Modeling Agency of New

York City, came up to Barbara and asked her to come to New York and work in her modeling agency. Barbara had just graduated from high school and Mrs. Ford said she could live in her home. So in that one fell swoop, Barbara removed the ugliest urchin on Earth false belief from her consciousness and became a model in New York in the most famous modeling agency of them all at the time.

Barbara's career as a model began having traction right away but by the end of the Fall of that year, 1971, she knew for sure that she needed to use her mind, and not her body, to make her way in the world. With money in the bank and a new outlook on life, Barbara entered Louisiana State University (L.S.U.) in January of 1972.

From Physicality to Spirituality

Two things immediately happened to Barbara when she went to L.S.U. First, she was introduced to Campus Crusade for Christ by a male classmate and became immersed in it. Second, she wanted to be a cheerleader but failed the tryouts.

When Barbara tried out for cheerleader at L.S.U. in 1972 she was an accomplished cheerleader and had been head cheerleader at her high school in New Orleans. And she was quite poised after having been personally groomed and trained by Eileen Ford. Since she started college in the spring, she practiced for months on her cheering and gymnastics skills before the summer tryouts. She even persuaded one of the male cheerleaders on the squad to coach her prior to the tryouts.

When her tryout came, to her amazement, her body wouldn't work. As hard as she tried, she couldn't make her hands clap together or even slap her side. She said it was as if she was a marionette and someone else was pulling the strings. You can imagine how shocked and totally embarrassed she was. And, of course, you know the result of her tryout.

As devastated as she was, she knew almost immediately that there was a reason for her not being able to perform at her tryout. She was a very natural and intuitive person and she could feel the intervention that was happening to her. She let go completely and just trusted and almost immediately she met a whole new set of friends whose path was a stepping stone to her own ultimate version of spirituality. And that is how Barbara learned to trust her inner guidance, a guidance that never failed her throughout the rest of her life. It was also the beginning steps on a spiritual path that Barbara would walk the rest of her life, although the nature and character of it changed over time.

One of the greatest lessons Barbara taught me, as her partner and best friend, was to live from the depths of my being, instead of from the conditioning of my mind, so that I could follow my inner guidance. In the cheerleading example, Barbara had been well conditioned, and socialized, about the admiration and adoration that college kids had for cheerleaders. But in that holy instant of "failure", she accepted herself exactly as she was and saw the experience simply as an experience, without any judgment at all. Looking back on it, she told me that must have been when she began to learn about self-love and self-acceptance. The experience was so severe she knew she had two choices. One choice was to judge herself, and the experience, as a failure and to carry that with her for the rest of her life. The other choice was to love and accept herself, and the experience, just as it was. She chose the latter.

Our Physical and Inner Attraction

To make up for lost time starting a semester late at L.S.U. Barbara would take 21 hours per semester, plus she went to summer school. She majored in microbiology *and* chemistry. She wanted to be a doctor. She made all A's in school and graduated Magna Cum Laude. In between the fall and spring semester of her sophomore year she was accepted to a branch of the L.S.U. medical school. However, by the time she graduated, she had fallen in love with a young missionary that was affiliated with Campus Crusade for Christ. Both he, and the overall Christian community in which she was now a part of and immersed in, had strong beliefs that a wife should not work outside of the home. So Barbara cancelled medical school and married the missionary. A couple of years later that missionary became a sales associate in my real estate company in Baton Rouge.

When I first met Barbara, sometime in 1976, I was introduced to her in my office by her husband who now worked in my real estate company. He left the room to check on some business, and I remember being taken immediately by her inner spirit, both drawn to her and taking her in at the same time. I couldn't define it, I couldn't name it, but I knew it was there: an attraction that would simmer, much like a pilot light on a heater or a fireplace that would hold the space of love for us until it would fully ignite 12 years later. It was not a sexual attraction, even though it had the full force of a sexual attraction. It was an attraction to Barbara's inner and outer radiance. It was absolutely magnificent.

Years later, as Barbara travelled in her job as a District Manager for a pharmaceutical company, there would always be one man, always a different stranger, she would tell me about that had spoken to her on the airplane, or elevator or hotel and they always said, in essence, the same thing: "You are so radiant. You light up the room" or some version of that. Barbara really was that radiant. She loved life and it showed.

Years later Barbara told me that when she met me in my office in 1976 she thought I was the best looking man she had ever seen. Of course I was flattered but I wonder if that is what was necessary to spark Barbara's interest in me so that the flame would ignite 12 years later. I know I unconsciously believed in those days that a man had to have a certain kind of look to be successful in business and in life. I don't believe that any more, of course, and I now believe that literally everyone is beautiful, and that beauty is in the eye of the beholder. But maybe I needed that cer-tain look so that Barbara could re-ignite that attraction years later when we met again as single people. Hers was a physical attraction that grew into including an inner attraction for me. Mine was an inner attraction that grew to include a physical attraction for her.

A New Spiritual Path

Barbara reached a point with her first husband where she felt like they were pulling in two different directions, the direction of responsibility on her part and the non-direction of irresponsibility on his part. She went to her pastor for counseling and advice. She was told that she "had" to remain in the marriage because of the teaching of the Bible about husband and wife. And she was told by every one of her friends, in that closely-knit Christian community, that she "had" to stay with her husband because of the Christian teachings. She felt trapped and didn't know where to turn so she did what she always did and turned to God.

In Baton Rouge there are two bridges over the Mississippi River, the old bridge and the new bridge. It was common back then, in the mid-70's, for people to say they felt like "jumping off the bridge", meaning the newer and larger one, when they were having a problem. Barbara's problem felt insurmountable to her because the entire Christian community in which she was enmeshed, the pastor himself, and the revered holy Bible, all were saying that it was her duty as a Christian to stay in the marriage. She told me she was suicidal and literally thought about "jumping off the bridge". That is when she turned to God.

Barbara went to the private place in her home where she prayed when she knew she would be the only one in the house. She got down on all fours, as she always did back then, and put her head down into her hands on the floor and prayed deeply. In the depth of that prayer she had the insight that her worldly father, who she knew loved her deeply, would not want her to remain in a marriage where she could not experience love. And then she realized that if her earthly father would not want her to remain in the marriage, how much more her heavenly Father would not want her to remain since His love was immeasurable and only wanted the best for her. In that moment she felt God's deep abiding love for her. And in the experience of that communion with God, Barbara knew that the self-loving thing to do was to leave the marriage. She filed for divorce and left the marriage immediately. And her spiritual path now took a whole new direction, free of rules and doctrine and concepts, and based solely on her personal relationship with God.

A Lifetime Promise

Part of Barbara's nature was that she was intrinsically non-judgmental. So when she saw a person, she didn't judge anything about their personal appearance or uniqueness. It was one of the main things that I liked about Barbara. Anyway, when I asked her why her second marriage was to a man many years older than her, she said she never gave his age a second thought. This was a short marriage, but one with a powerful lesson. In short, Barbara was kind of like a Barbie doll in this relationship or eye candy for her husband.

At first it was subtle and flattering, but eventually this focus erupted into Barbara realizing there was nothing in the relationship but a physical focus. And, when Barbara began to speak up about that to her husband, he became verbally, emotionally and physically abusive. When he finally threatened her by raising a gun to her head, she knew it was over and she slipped out one morning never to return. As soon as she was free and had space to reflect on what had happened, she went deep inside and made a promise to herself that "I would never put myself down or ever let anyone else put me down". She kept and honored that promise the rest of her life.

Nature Abhors a Vacuum

Her final relationship before me was immediately after her second marriage. The one thing Barbara told me she always wanted in her life was to have a deeply meaningful loving relationship. After the second husband, she was so beaten up and bruised emotionally that she consciously let go of the idea of ever finding a love relationship. And, true to form, the old truism that "nature abhors a vacuum" took over immediately. She was dragged to a party by an old girlfriend and there she met a man that she thought was the man of her dreams. The chemistry was instant and she jumped into the relationship immediately, completely convinced that she had found the man of her dreams. He was different and unique and everything that Barbara unconsciously thought she was not. The romance and relationship was intense but peaked quickly.

On another beach in Hawaii with this man they used MDMA but he immediately said he only wanted to read the novel he had brought for the trip. Barbara's intuition told her that he was hiding something and knew he didn't want to delve into a deep discussion on MDMA or he might expose whatever he was hiding. She walked down that literally and symbolically black beach and crashed into a heap of despair, heightened by the reverse effect of the normally love-inducing MDMA into a depression unlike any she had ever felt. The words came to her: "You come into this world alone and you leave alone". And, in that moment, she decided she was meant to live a life without a partner, without the love relationship that she had so long sought after.

Within weeks Barbara discovered her relationship partner was having an affair and she left the relationship and moved into a small apartment since they jointly owned the house. She called her boss and asked him to send her to a pharmaceutical convention anywhere, as soon as possible. She just wanted to get away. He said he had one coming up in Manhattan and she said, "I'll take it".

Barbara called her friend, Phyllis, my sister, who lived in Manhattan and told her she was coming to a convention and could she come for a visit when it was over that weekend. That was February, 1988. I had been living with Phyllis for six months when Barbara made that call. In March, Barbara came back for a second visit and I picked her up at the airport. We were now living in Westchester County, New York, but Barbara and I were so engrossed in our new connection with each other that I drove right past Westchester and ended up somewhere in northern Connecticut before I realized we were literally lost in conversation. The rest is history.

My Early Life

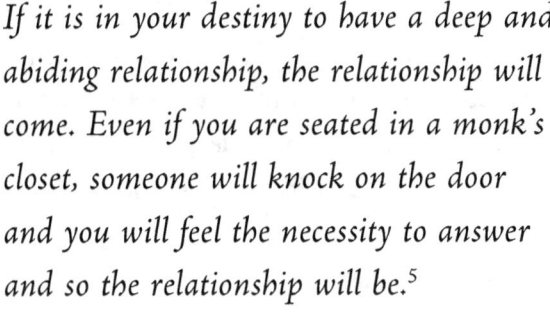

If it is in your destiny to have a deep and abiding relationship, the relationship will come. Even if you are seated in a monk's closet, someone will knock on the door and you will feel the necessity to answer and so the relationship will be.[5]

—Bartholomew

Barbara and I lived in the same house that she and her last boyfriend lived in and owned. We bought his half interest in the house and it became ours. Barbara loved the house. She said it "hugged her". It was a beautiful, Swiss chalet type of house, with huge spacious rooms, full of glass and made of Louisiana cypress. We lived on an acre of land out in the countryside outside of New Orleans.

A Repressed Memory

One morning I was peacefully driving to work. I believe the drive was so peaceful that it acted as a mantra for my mind to be completely relaxed and receptive. I also believe that I was ready, finally mature enough, to learn what I was going to learn about myself during this drive. As I slowly rounded a bend of the Mississippi River along that country river road, I suddenly remembered, out of nowhere, an event that I would later figure out happened when I was about six years old. As I was driving, I saw myself asleep in my bed with my younger brother, Brad, on the other side of the room asleep in his. Our younger sister, Phyllis, was asleep in her room between ours and our parents.

I saw that I was having a dream, actually a nightmare, where a huge ball of blackness was getting larger and larger and was swirling around getting closer and closer to me. It felt like the end of the world. And then, just as the blackness was about to engulf me, I ever so slowly awakened to realize that the roaring sound I had been hearing from the blackness was actually my Mom and Dad screaming and hollering at each other in the kitchen. My Dad had come home drunk. Mom was furious and my Dad was verbally fighting back. My one and only thought was a terror that they would wake up, and terrify, Brad and Phyllis. Then, in what felt like a full moment of deep depression, I felt myself sigh and fall asleep. I kept driving for a few seconds, perhaps a minute or two, and then a second memory came to me which was exactly like the first. My Dad coming home drunk, and my Mom and Dad fighting, had happened twice.

It took me a long time to figure out how that experience of my Mom and Dad fighting had changed me, but I did figure it out. It took much, much longer to change my beliefs about myself that those two experiences stimulated me into believing about myself.

I have known for a long time that what was a traumatic experience for me as a six year old was exactly what I needed to facilitate the kind of overall life experience that I am here to have. The pain of that experience was exactly what I needed to eventually propel me onto my spiritual path. I, of course, have no judgment whatsoever about my Mom and Dad fighting those two nights. And I am grateful for the perfect role they played as my parents that was such an important part in my spiritual awakening.

I found pictures of myself as a child where I was happy and carefree. But the annual class pictures from the Catholic elementary school that I attended were a dead giveaway. My first grade picture reflected a happy, unconcerned five year old with a crooked tie and rumpled shirt. My second grade picture was quite different. And so were every other picture every year after that. My second grade picture showed a very serious little boy, all prim and proper, with perfectly straight tie and unwrinkled shirt. But the most outstanding difference between the two pictures was the carefree smile of the first grader and the somber, serious frown of the second grader.

Waking up to my parents fighting and screaming at each other was an experience that I internalized as "there must be something wrong with me or they would not have terrified me like that. I must not be good enough or they would have done something to protect me from being terrified". And, "I must not be lovable or they would have loved me enough to have protected me in some way". In that moment of falling back to sleep deeply depressed, with a huge sigh, I had created for myself those inner, unconscious beliefs about myself and the emotion of that was deep, abiding shame. I learned in a recovery workshop once, around 1990, from the author John Bradshaw, that guilt was the belief that I did something wrong and shame was the belief that there was something wrong with me. And that is how I felt.

From Little Boy to Perfectionist

I also became a perfectionist in that moment of depression as I went back to sleep. I didn't know that for years, but that is what it was. And I did a great job at being a perfectionist. I became the youngest altar boy in the St. Anthony of Padua Catholic Church in Eunice, Louisiana, thanks to my maternal grandfather, a patron of the church. I trained with a beginning group of altar boys all of whom were in the fifth grade. I was in the third. I was terrified and didn't know what I was doing, but I did it. And from then on I did everything early in life, like going into business for myself. And I always did it well.

I peaked at doing everything well in my early 30's. I had a real estate company with 26 sales associates, one of whom was Barbara's first husband, and a staff of six administrative people. And I was emotionally suffocating and felt like I was in prison. From the moment of that six year old experience, I quit seeing the world through my own eyes and saw the world only through the eyes of the world. I did what I thought I *should* do. I became who I thought I *should* be.

I wanted everyone to love and admire me so I treated everyone in a way that would result in getting love and admiration back from them. In short, I projected my terror of the world, based on the shame-based sense of self that I had, onto the world. I then defended myself from that terror-filled world through a perfectionistic approach to life. I did that by giving, which was actually taking, to everyone in my life what I thought they needed and wanted in order for them to like, love and admire me. I had completely lost my sense of self and was suffocating, or drowning, in the pain of feeling imprisoned by an unrelenting drive to be successful so that I would be admired and respected. My shattered sense of self was desperately trying to create it's perfect opposite self out in the world.

I then unconsciously destroyed my real estate company, did crazy things to just tear it apart, in a desperate attempt to get the inner freedom that I was really seeking. In one fell swoop, during the first week of September, 1980, two major things happened to me at the same time. While my real estate company began to crumble before my very eyes, my little brother, Ferdie, came running into my office with a copy of *Autobiography of a Yogi*, by Paramahansa Yogananda, talking to me about past lives and reincarnation.

My perfectionism and sense of total responsibility for everything and everyone around me crumbled and transformed into an aversion toward responsibility and a fearful sense that I couldn't do anything anymore. I became obsessive, worried and consciously afraid of everything. At the same time I had a deep sense that there was something true and real about this alternative version of spirituality that I was being introduced to. It instantly resonated with me. As my real estate company crumbled, I began a whole new journey on what I could see was the beginning of my spiritual path.

A New Me

In the turmoil and new beginnings of that first week in September of 1980, I felt like my mind had broken open and from that moment on I had, and still have, a clear, felt-sense of when I am in ego and when I am not. The ego part felt like a continuation of what I had always been, like the same old "me". The non-ego part felt like an inner clarity, a sense of peace and a wisdom that just knew what to do versus the old me that always tried to figure out what to do and how to be. At the time, I mostly felt confused and afraid with moments of clarity breaking through in pressure situations. It would take years for me to learn what this really was and to trust and act on the new intuitive me that had opened up from deep within.

I spent the next seven years trying desperately to work as a real estate salesperson in my now greatly reduced company of four salespeople: myself, my second wife, and two loyal associates from my previously much larger company. Everyone else moved on to do something else in their life once my co-dependent, perfectionistic support had crumbled beneath them.

My first marriage, with one child, had disintegrated and two years later, in 1980, I married my top salesperson. Seven years later, as I sat across my second wife's desk complaining and moaning in misery about still being in real estate, she said to me, "Why don't you get out of real estate?" I was shocked. I had never thought of that, just like I had never thought of leaving my first wife. It took her to ask me to leave. Now my second wife was giving me permission to walk away from real estate. She said she made enough money for both of us, which she did. I walked out of my real estate company that day never to return. I then spent most of the next year trying to do inspirational public speaking and training when I could barely keep my eyes open because I was so depressed. I was down and felt like a failure.

In Movement

Out of nowhere, my sister Phyllis, now living in Manhattan, called and asked me to move up there and live with her. She had had enough phone conversations with me to know that I was deeply depressed and she sincerely wanted to help me. I told her I'd think about it. When I told my wife about Phyllis' idea, she said, "Well, you've done everything you can do here. It sounds like a good idea." Within a few days I was on my way to Manhattan with only $200 in my pocket. Within a few months, my wife and I realized that we had grown apart and quite happily agreed to officially separate. A couple of years later, when I first moved back to Baton Rouge to live with Barbara, she and I met my second wife at the courthouse where we happily went through the divorce proceedings. I did all the paper work and acted as the lawyer for my wife and I and we were, in fact, happily divorced. I've never seen a marriage end so happily. We had and have mutual love and respect for each other and both moved on to new lives.

I moved in with Phyllis on my brother Brad's birthday, July 22, 1987. I had a bedroom to myself. I slept on a mattress on the floor. And my "chest of drawers" was shoe boxes. I had no idea where I was headed, but I was in movement. Barbara came to Manhattan for that convention in February of 1988. I moved in with Barbara on Phyllis' birthday, August 4, 1988. Our holy relationship had begun. We just didn't know it.

Fear Creeps In

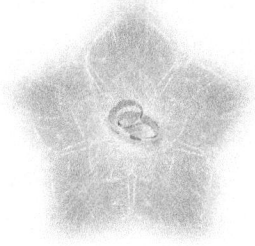

Remember that where your heart is, there is your treasure also ... Everyone defends his treasure, and will do so automatically. The real questions are, what do you treasure and how much do you treasure it?[6]
— A Course in Miracles

On our way back from that first trip to Hawaii in May of 1988 we had a several hour layover at the LAX airport. It was around midnight and we were both tired and feeling ragged. Since she was so tired, Barbara asked me to call her business voicemail for her and just tell her what the messages were. As I got up to the pay phone (no cell phones then) I could feel a surge of fear coming up from deep within me. The fear was stimulated by my surface tiredness, but it was really rooted in my fear that I was not enough and that I *had* to make the phone call for Barbara or I would be risking her leaving me. I didn't know that at the time, but that's what it was. And as an extension of that fear I felt anger toward Barbara for asking me to make that call.

Anger was a stranger to me. I very rarely experienced it and then only when I felt attacked by someone. This was way more subtle. I was attacking myself, being angry at myself for making a phone call I didn't want to make and projecting that unwanted anger onto Barbara. I was shocked and stunned as I absorbed the fear and anger as I made that call. I was self-aware enough to recognize my old friend, fear, and I silently labeled it ego and sighed in a quiet knowing that my ego had already made its way into my relationship with Barbara. Just as our holy relationship began on that beach in Hawaii, the pain of our relationship began in that phone booth in the Los Angeles airport.

After I arrived back in Manhattan and Barbara in New Orleans, I called her every night and one of us flew to see the other each weekend. We truly had a long distance relationship. I used to love picking her up at the Manhattan airport and to be greeted by her at the New Orleans airport. On my first trip to New Orleans after our Hawaii experience, we kissed in the terminal and she said, "Have you ever noticed how our lips fit perfectly together?" I said, "Yes". Our whole relationship felt like that, that we fit perfectly together.

Being Watered with Love

It didn't take long before we removed the physical distance in our relationship. I soon helped Barbara move from that small apartment in New Orleans back to the house she owned in Baton Rouge. In her wisdom, she wanted to be away from the energy and location of her last two relationships, the boyfriend and her second husband. In a bathtub in that house on Heatherwood Drive in Baton Rouge, Barbara asked me, "Why don't you move in with me?" I sat there in amazement, then wonder, as I felt an intuition arise within me that I expressed verbally as I held both arms out to the side to represent the two opposites I was expressing: "I can stay in Manhattan and continue my business career. Or I can move in with you and be watered by your love. I'll take the watering." I gave two week's notice at my job and after only ten weeks from our Hawaii experience, moved in with Barbara. What began then was the first trial of our holy relationship.

Mental versus Emotional

Barbara had given herself so wholly to her relationship with her last boyfriend that it was hard for her to let go of him. One of Barbara's strongest characteristics was the command she had over her mind. She used it wisely and adroitly to maneuver her way through life. It was very powerful because she exercised it in a very powerful way. In this case, she knew intellectually to leave the boyfriend, and did, but the emotional sense of love and attachment was still stuck in her heart. To complicate matters worse, he immediately regretted losing her and proposed marriage over the telephone to her, which she declined immediately. Her decision to leave him was final. Her emotions were not.

Even though we moved from New Orleans to Baton Rouge, Barbara's pharmaceutical territory still included New Orleans and her old boyfriend knew her work routine well and always called her frequently to meet her in New Orleans. Barbara didn't allow quiet, intimate dinners with him, but did agree to see him occasionally at his office. She was also having a hard time seeing his pain of losing her and she was trying to let him down gently.

I was aware of all of this and cringed every time the phone rang because I was afraid it would be him and it often was. I didn't answer the phone much back then and never did have to take one of his calls. This went on for about six months. And the symbol of it continuing was that Barbara had promised to finish a stained glass piece for him that she began as a gift for him toward the end of their relationship. To make the process go quicker, Barbara taught me how to do stained glass and on several occasions I would be doing the stained glass project while she was in New Orleans with him for an hour or so at the end of the day before she drove home to Baton Rouge. These trips were not quite as frequent as they sound, but there were several visits between Barbara and the ex-boyfriend.

As you can imagine, I was in pain over this. And to make it even more painful, the ex-boyfriend told Barbara that I "was a loser", which went right down to my lack of self-worth issue. However, even with all of this stirred up inside of me, I *knew*, somewhere very deep down inside of me, like an intuitive knowing, the value of my relationship with Barbara. And, because of that, I opened my heart wide open and made the decision to give Barbara literally all the time she needed to have a completion of the old relationship.

I was feeling the emotional pain of Barbara being with this hero of a kind of guy, with a Psy.D. and a great job, and a uniqueness that I could relate to and was jealous of. I was unemployed, working to build an entrepreneurial consulting practice and feeling afraid and unstable. But a larger part of me had a sense of knowing that my inner worth was exactly what Barbara needed and wanted and it was in that knowing that I was able to both allow the pain I was feeling and hold the space of our relationship for as long as it took for Barbara to get to completion with her ex-boyfriend. We finished the stained glass piece. Barbara arranged to bring it to him and that was the last time she ever saw him. That era was over in our lives.

My Treasure

How does this relate to a holy relationship? The main thing I learned from our experience with the ex-boyfriend was the tremendous sense of value that I had for Barbara. I *knew* I wanted to be with her, without a shadow of a doubt. And it wasn't so much Barbara the person as it was the spirit of Barbara. For example, about six months after we had been living together in our Heatherwood house in Baton Rouge, I got out of bed, where we had just had a wonderful sexual experience together, and as I was walking around the foot of the bed and looking back at Barbara, I realized something and stopped in my tracks and told her, "Wow! You really have a beautiful body. I fell in love with your spirit. It seems like I just now noticed your body for the first time." I know that might sound ridiculous, but that's exactly how I felt at that time. Sure, I had noticed her body before and yes we had had wonderful sexual experiences together before that, but I had never really given much thought, or recognition, or value, to her body as in that moment. I truly did fall in love with Barbara's spirit. It was like my spirit resonated deeply with hers. And that was our bond. That is what always got us through all challenges and turmoil.

Our Eyes on Each Other

To have a holy relationship you have to value the other person the same way you value yourself. Or, to say it in reverse, to have a holy relationship you have to value yourself the same way you value the other person. You are not more special than the other person. The other person is not more special than you. In fact, there is no specialness between you at all. It is, rather, a sense of oneness, a union, a joining of one with the other.

Our prayer/affirmation about each other, which was the essence of those first recommitment vows that we practiced for years, was that we "wanted to know the other as ourself and ourself as the other". And this required what we called "having our eyes on each other". We believed that love was attention and that we placed our attention on what we value and what we value is what we love.

Barbara taught me all of this. And it took me a long time to learn it and to live it. That was because I was very self-focused at the beginning of our relationship because I was so terrified of life inside and therefore always defending against the perceived fear and pain of life by being self-focused. My self-focus became the focus of Barbara's pain in our relationship. Barbara's pain became the stimulus of my fear of losing her.

A Bottom-Line Relationship

Barbara's challenge was to love herself enough to stand up for herself, to keep that old promise that she made to herself, and she did it beautifully and uncompromisingly. Our challenges, our disagreements, our arguments, our pain, were all always bottom-line for us because Barbara always insisted on receiving love from me or her self-love dictated that she leave the relationship. I know that might be disturbing to you, instead of the more blind belief that marriage vows will carry a couple into and throughout a lifetime of bliss and love.

Barbara and I had each been married twice, had each experienced two sets of marriage vows and learned a lot from both of our previous marriages and relationships. This time we wanted reality. We wanted truth. We really did want love. Barbara insisted on it and I rose to the occasion. It was like the "razor's edge" of Zen, always living razor sharp in the giving and receiving of love, in the keen awareness of love, in the enjoyment of love so that, if fear slipped in from either of us, we were able to recognize it right away and deal with it head-on. From our study of Zen, not only did we appreciate living on the razor's edge in the fullness of the moment, but also living on the razor's edge in our relationship. That meant to us that it took conscious choice and decision to choose love as many times as necessary so as to not fall off of the razor's edge of love in our relationship and to ultimately have those choices and decisions transformed into an easy and effortless way of life for us.

My challenge was to love Barbara more than my fear. And because I did love her more than my fear, because I did value her more than my fear, I always rose to the occasion and made a substantive change in my belief system when we had conflict and that allowed us to move into a deeper and more expansive love than we had before the conflict. It was like I went from kindergarten through a Ph.D. in love during the 22 years of our relationship. It was a beautiful and exquisite process of growth and unfolding, incredibly painful at times, but beautiful and exquisite nonetheless.

Vehicle for Love

Do you see how, in these two examples of the respective challenges for Barbara and me, that our relationship served as the vehicle to facilitate love? It was the perfect vehicle for our personalities and, I believe, that all relationships are for, regardless of the types of personalities that are in any given relationship. There are no accidents in the universe. We each attract into our lives the very person we need so that we can best learn about love. Sometimes, and quite often, that means leaving a relationship in order to choose self-love. Sometimes, and quite often, that means losing a relationship and having the pain of fear increase in order to become more attracted to love.

I was the stimulus in Barbara's life to challenge her to love herself enough to risk losing our relationship. Had she not done that, we would have been stuck in fear. Barbara was the stimulus in my life to choose love of Barbara over my fear. Had I not done that, we would have been stuck in fear.

Mindfulness and the Razor's Edge

We used a combination of Far Eastern and Western mindfulness to keep us on the "razor's edge". Far Eastern mindfulness taught us to be fully present with each other in each moment. Western mindfulness, which we learned from the work of Ellen Langer, Ph.D., of Harvard, taught us how to not take each other for granted. By combining the two, we had a deep appreciation for each other as we were, right here, right now, and a keen awareness that we were both always changing, even though it may appear almost imperceptible to the naked eye or unaware observer. That caused us to invoke creative questions about each other continually which, in turn, always revealed something new about what was going on in each of our creative minds and, thus, how we were changing. It also taught us to listen to the other with our hearts and minds wide open to receive and to actually hear what we were listening to from the other. Our relationship was alive and vibrant.

Knowing and Being Known

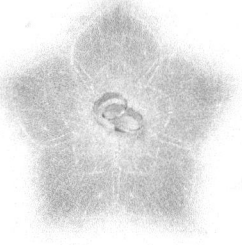

Love wishes to be known, completely understood and shared. It has no secrets; nothing it would keep apart and hide.[7]
— A Course in Miracles

To know and be known is perhaps the most wonderful feeling that any two people can feel for each other. Barbara began teaching me that the first time we went out to dinner after we moved in together. She loved Mexican food and we were at a new Mexican restaurant that an old acquaintance of mine had recently opened and that seemed to be thriving. The place was lively, everyone seemed happy and

Barbara and I were madly in love with each other. I felt great. That is until she began telling me that it would hurt us to keep secrets from each other and that it would help us in our intimacy to be completely open and honest with each other.

I didn't know why, but deep down I felt afraid, like I was hiding something, but I didn't know what it was. And it felt like if I did know that I wouldn't want to tell her because it might cause her to leave me. Then she said, "You can always tell me anything. It doesn't matter what it is. No matter how bad it is, we can always work it out if we just talk to each other and work it out together." All of a sudden something changed inside of me and I felt open and free. I was actually happy to have heard what she just said. I now knew that whatever I might be hiding would only hurt me to keep it inside. And I realized in that instant that by being able to totally reveal myself to Barbara, and her accept me the way I was, no matter what, I would then be able to accept myself. And that felt wonderful. It felt liberating. I said, "That sounds great. And you can always tell me anything also. No matter what it is, we'll always work it out." And we always did.

Love and Acceptance

So in that moment, in that holy instant of connected communication, locked eye-to-eye and fully present for each other and with each other, we added to our spiritual path as a couple the value that we would always love and accept each other, just the way we were. That was way more delicious than the great meal we were having. And it was priceless. I was to learn through this process of being open and honest with each other that I had been hiding a whole cluster of false beliefs about myself, all of which were the cause of every adult emotional pain I had ever had. It felt like I was a bird let out of a cage and I hadn't even begun to discover, much less reveal, what I had been hiding. But the process had begun.

The Rooteralliduck

The process actually began on that first Hawaii trip when we realized that we both felt so comfortable with each other because we were really being ourselves with each other. We were teaching each other, without even realizing it, that by being ourselves with each other we become more comfortable with each other and more trusting of each other and, as a result, more comfortable with, and trusting of, ourselves.

That was something that we saw we wanted in our relationship, something that we valued, and we knew it was good for both of us. And then we stumbled upon what would become known to us as the "rooteralliduck". It was a most unusual original ceramic piece designed to look like a combination of several different animals made all into one: a rooster, an alligator and a duck. We both fell in love with it and bought it on the spot right there in the village of Hanalei, on the island of Kauai, the garden island of Hawaii. Our rooteralliduck symbolized to us that we could each be our unique selves, and honor and accept the uniqueness in each of us, without any judgment or criticism for, after all, who really knows how a rooteralliduck is "supposed" to act except a rooteralliduck?

I broke the rooteralliduck once because of my slip-shod (this is not a judgment, just an observation; do you see how that works?) packing during one of our many moves from house to house. When I saw the break I immediately related it to me and that I must be hiding something from Barbara, not being authentic with her. I was right. So I exposed it, talked about it with Barbara, changed my mind about the need to be hiding that aspect of myself, and then let it go. We also fixed the rooteralliduck and it looked like new, which is how I felt inside.

Then I began to really open to my vulnerability as a vehicle for self-acceptance.

The Power of Vulnerability

My first introduction to the idea of the power of vulnerability was during a very sacred year that I spent as a member of an A.C.O.A. (Adult Children of Alcoholics) group in Baton Rouge. I started with Al Anon but quickly moved to A.C.O.A. and found a home there. Working backwards from the time I moved to Manhattan, I spent about a year going to those A.C.O.A. meetings every week, Monday through Friday. They were noon meetings and I loved going. I found my "voice" there. I was able to communicate about myself, as myself, and could tell that I was beginning the process of unwinding the conditioning that had kept me in a co-dependent attachment to what the outside world, other people, thought of me. It was like finding a clear stream of pure, healthy water in the middle of the desert.

One day, in one of those A.C.O.A. meetings, a female in the group about my age, around 40, told us that sometimes she would get so afraid when she was out in the world that she would find a public bathroom somewhere and pull out a pacifier that she used to calm herself with. The pacifier was an idea her therapist had come up with. Her being able to open up to a room full of strangers, except that we were a family who all only had a first name, during that one hour every day, is a testament to the level of intimacy and trust that we had created in that sacred environment that was labeled an A.C.O.A. meeting to the outside world. The woman continued with her story and said something that resonated deeply within me, something that I will never forget, and something that changed me forever. She told us that her therapist had taught her to "go to the heart of your fear and there you will find safety". I knew in an instant that that was true. My heart flung wide open and my mind knew that I had learned something that would help me, and it did.

What I learned in that A.C.O.A. meeting that day is that in our vulnerability lies our power. In human terms, invulnerability implies bravado, or a false sense of power, which is made up in our minds and projected out into the world as a defense against us, or anyone else, ever finding out what it is that we're all hiding about ourselves deep down inside of ourselves. And there is a paradox, or truism, in all of this.

The Power of Paradox

I learned what a paradox is in the mid-1970's. In that moment, when I realized that a paradox is really the opposite of what something seems to be, my heart again flung wide open and the idea of paradox resonated deeply inside of me. From that moment on, I have always looked at paradoxes carefully and to this day I have always found truth hiding within a paradox.

So paradoxes are very important to me. I now know that they resonate so deeply within me because the whole idea of "human race consciousness", or what I call "race consciousness" for short, which is how we humans see the world, is, paradoxically, the opposite of how it really is. And in this example of being vulnerable, the paradox is that the more we hide our fears inside of the deep unconscious recesses of our mind, the greater they become. It is our belief that what we are hiding can hurt us that actually hurts us. It is the belief we have about ourselves that we are unlovable or not enough or any other fearful belief about ourselves, that hurts us. And, paradoxically, the more energy we use to cover up and hide our false beliefs from ourselves, the fear gets stronger and the more it hurts us. Conversely, when we are vulnerable enough to open ourselves wide open and look at our fears, paradoxically, the fear begins to dissipate, to dissolve and to be transformed into a new, truthful awareness about our inner strength, the core essence of every living being that lies underneath our deepest fear.

And that is why openness, or the willingness to be vulnerable with our partner, is, paradoxically, a major facilitator of healing in a holy relationship. If the receiving partner of our vulnerability accepts and loves us unconditionally as we share our vulnerability in the form of revealing a fear-based false belief about ourselves, a joining is created that facilitates healing in both partners. Done together, continually, both partners in the relationship are able to heal old, childhood wounds. The holy relationship becomes a receptacle of transformation for psychological wounds to be healed. False beliefs and doubts become truth and certainty. Fear becomes love. Because of this, holy relationships don't break. They become stronger. Instead of having a foundation of fear, there is a foundation of love interwoven into, and as, the relationship.

Hidden False Beliefs

A hidden false belief is actually a psychological defense mechanism that we unconsciously create so that we cannot feel the emotional pain of the false belief. We create defense mechanisms within ourselves in order to hide unbearable emotional pain when we are very young and not mature enough mentally or emotionally to process the pain. By the time we are adults, we have avoided the awareness of the hidden emotional pain, and causative false beliefs about ourself, for so long that the pain becomes unbearable and comes out in our relationships with other people.

When the false belief is stimulated by a partner in a committed couple relationship, the energy of it feels like an aversion to whatever the partner is saying or doing or not saying or not doing. Since the partner is the one doing the stimulating, and the aversion is so painful, the partner with the false belief attributes the pain to the other partner. The pained partner becomes the victim of the other partner. The pained partner blames the other partner for the pain. But the problem, and the solution, are all wrapped up inside of the unconscious mind of the partner with the false belief. And it is this kind of unexamined pain that leads to couples breaking up and going their separate ways, only to find someone else to project their problems onto.

Core Issue and Primal Fear

In our work as psychotherapists, specializing in relationships and couple counseling, literally every partner in a couple relationship that we ever worked with was hiding something about themself that they believed would cause their partner to leave them if the partner knew about it. With every couple that worked with us long enough, each partner would eventually reveal this to us, either in a private one-on-one session (Barbara and I always worked together as co-therapists, so it was us with one of the partners) or right there in front of the other partner.

And, with those couples that did work with us at that depth, each one of them individually ultimately revealed, in a fully present, holy instant of honesty, usually crying their eyes out, some core, bottom-line belief about themself that was their core issue from childhood that had been unconsciously running their lives for years. They had been hiding this core issue from their partner because they were afraid that if their partner knew they had that core issue, that the partner would leave them. They had been hiding this core issue from themself since childhood because, as a child, they were not mature enough to address that issue. Now, as an adult, in that therapeutic environment, the core issue always came out. That core issue was the most distilled down issue of all their issues. That core issue was always a false belief about themself. And that false belief about themself was terrifying to them.

When I discovered my core issue, that there was something wrong with me, and the fear that it produced, I decided then and there to call it "primal fear". It is this primal fear that a holy relationship is able to dissolve and transform into unadulterated, unconditional love and acceptance of oneself and your partner. And if that is not holy, and sacred, then nothing is.

Into-Me-See

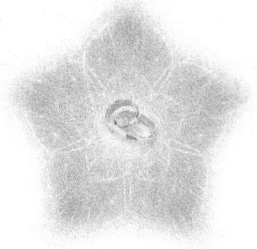

This thing of darkness I acknowledge mine.[8]

—SHAKESPEARE

Barbara taught me that intimacy means "into-me-see". And the best example I have of the bravery, honesty and openness of intimacy was also the scariest one for me. There was a time in our relationship, early on, when we seemed to be moving forward, like couples do, living life together with everything "seeming" to be just fine. By now I was beginning to develop my intuition and I had a sense, just barely underneath the surface of my consciousness, of something not being quite right with our relationship. But I hadn't developed enough confidence in our "knowing and being known" process, or in myself as Barbara's equal partner, to speak up about it. Barbara didn't have that kind of cloudiness in her mind and one night, at dinner, she spoke up about it. "Jimmie, I want to talk to you about something."

Since I knew something was off about us, and since I was still carrying fear around in my consciousness, I felt deep down that I was "guilty" of something, that it was my "fault" for whatever was wrong with us. I use quotation marks here to illustrate that I was still carrying around judgment in my mind which is where the made-up ideas, or mental constructs, of guilt, fault, and blame come from.

A Chill of Fear

I felt a chill of fear run down my spine as Barbara continued. "I feel like you and I are not connected. And I'm speaking up because I don't want to start thinking about other men." This is the type of openness and honesty that Barbara and I had in our relationship. It took me a long time to get to her level, but each time we reached a stuck place in our relationship we would talk about it and get it resolved.

It was usually me that was hanging onto some kind of fear and I always had the choice of risking our relationship or choosing love instead of fear. And I always chose love because I knew what I had in Barbara, the love that she was, I knew intellectually the love that I was and I always knew that it was a choice between love and fear. And I'm happy to say that I always chose love. I'm also happy to say that it was always an easy, obvious choice for me. Letting go of old fears was painful, because I had to face them first, but I always knew that the pain of not letting go of my fear would cost me my relationship with Barbara. And because Barbara, and "us", represented my path to knowing God, I always had that value, that motivation, and the power of love behind my decisions to choose Barbara, "us" and love. I always chose "us", or love, over fear.

Barbara didn't have to threaten me with losing our relationship because we had talked about, and knew, that if we didn't have openness and honesty we wouldn't have love and if we didn't have love we wouldn't have a relationship. This is something we talked about and consciously knew and agreed on.

Unresolved False Beliefs

The intimacy of our discussion at the dinner table that night was initially a shock of terror inside of me because, even though our relationship was alive and vibrant, I still had unresolved false beliefs about myself that weakened my confidence in my ability to have a loving relationship with Barbara.

So talking to me about the possibility of her losing interest in me, and getting interested in other men, or another man, was terrifying. But it was exactly the stimulus I needed to wake up to another level of love in our relationship. This is a prime example of how couples, and really every person, always attract into their life the exact circumstance to best facilitate the openness to, and awareness of, love.

What I learned about myself is that I had fallen off the razor's edge of awareness and was taking Barbara, and our relationship, for granted. That night we both resolved to live "consciously" in our relationship and to not take each other, or our relationship, for granted. Notice the no-blame by Barbara of me and her co-responsibility in the matter since the issue was about "us" and because we saw all problems in our relationship as "our" problem. This type of joining was, I believe, another step toward, and into, the holy relationship that we were creating.

The Two-Step Tango: Barbara's Version

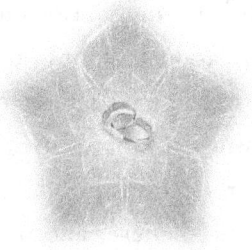

Projection makes the whole world a replica of our own unknown face.[9]
—CARL JUNG

Barbara and I went to graduate school later in life to become psychotherapists so that we could get her out of corporate America and have a professional expression more in line with our own natural proclivities toward self-awareness and personal growth. We chose Prescott College, of Prescott, Arizona, because of its unique approach to learning. Everything was experiential, practicing what you're learning, and the curriculum was designed by the student under the tutelage of a personal mentor as an academic advisor, along with a Ph.D. level core faculty overseeing the whole process.

We designed our curriculum to include all of the requirements to get licensed in the State of Texas because we lived in Houston. But around that core curriculum, we wrapped an expanded curriculum of couple counseling and transpersonal psychology. We compared our curriculum to the other schools that we considered and the number of books, research studies and other forms of learning that we were doing seemed to us to be about ten times more than the normal or average required reading and doing than at other schools. So it took us three years, instead of two, to work our way through this complex, but rewarding, curriculum. And we loved every minute of it.

Transpersonal Psychology

Transpersonal psychology emphasizes going *beyond* psychology, thus the prefix, "trans", meaning across, over or beyond traditional psychology. It takes psychology into the realm of the spiritual and becomes a psychospiritual approach to learning about yourself and others. We researched everything we could find about transpersonal psychology, along with everything we could find about spirituality, including all the ancient traditions and all contemporary approaches to spirituality. We had been doing this for years anyway, in our own search for truth and enlightenment, but now we did it with an academic zeal and a personal passion and fervor. We were on fire for learning. We wanted to learn about ourselves. We wanted to learn about each other. And we wanted to use what we learned to help other people in relationships, especially committed couple relationships.

Thesis Research

As the culminating work of our curriculum, we had to do a thesis project involving research with the demonstration and results of that research wrapped up in a formal thesis paper. Because our core faculty knew of our emphasis on working with couples, she recommended to us an approach to research where Barbara and I would actually do research on ourselves. This fit us perfectly. Barbara became the primary researcher for her thesis, with me as her co-researcher. I became the primary researcher for my thesis, with her as my co-researcher. In this way, we were able to do direct experiential research on ourselves personally and, at the same time, apply it to our relationship as a couple.

Barbara did her research on the psychological defense mechanism of projection because she knew that all humans project what they are hiding from themselves onto other people. She knew that couples did that to each other. And she knew that she did that to me. She wanted to remove projection from our relationship and to learn how to teach couples to quit projecting onto each other.

I did my research on the overall idea of psychological defense mechanisms because I knew that I had spent a lifetime of hiding my emotional pain deep inside of myself and, in so doing, hid myself from others and from myself. Because of that, I knew that I had created an innate tendency toward hiding and I wanted to reverse that and become completely open. I knew the pain of hiding and I wanted to know the power of openness. I knew everyone else had psychological defense mechanisms and I knew how painful they were to couples. I wanted to remove all defensiveness from myself and my relationship with Barbara and I wanted to learn how to teach couples to remove psychological defenses from their relationship.

One Step Pain, Two Step Blame

We saw that we had created a dance of pain in our relationship that we called the "two-step tango". The first step was when one of us felt any type of emotional pain within our relationship. The second step was that we immediately projected that pain onto the other person. Our pain became the "fault" of our partner. Our pain was "caused" by our partner. So we blamed our partner, overtly or covertly, as we danced around each other with our respective emotional pain that we were convinced was the result of our partner being "bad" or "wrong" about something. One step pain, two step blame. In combination, each partner dancing their own version of the two-step tango, partners end up with unbearable pain because each looks to the wrong source of the pain. The answer or solution is within each person, but the blame is on the other person. And this kind of pain comes out in all of the myriad ways couples act out this pain that ends up in stale relationships or no relationship at all.

We spent a year in research and working on our respective theses. I was teaching half-time and being a house husband half-time. Barbara was working full time as a pharmaceutical district manager working daily out in the field with one of a dozen sales representatives, with a lot of voicemails, faxes and paperwork after that. Barbara's weekdays were full. On Saturdays we saw clients in our home for the "practicum", or practice, part of our graduate work. And we had a local licensed supervisor working with us, looking over our shoulder and advising us on how to work with clients in the most healing and therapeutic way.

So we made the decision to use Sundays for our thesis research. You can see that we had very little personal time in those days. We committed to devoting as much as five hours on Sundays for our thesis research and were so engaged usually from noon to 5 P.M. every Sunday. Sometimes we would devote the whole time to Barbara's personal research into herself. Sometimes we would devote the whole time to my personal research into myself. And other times we would devote the whole time to ourselves as a couple. The one being the co-researcher would ask questions, push and prod, analyze, give feedback and suggestions and generally do everything possible to help the other one open fully to what was going on inside of the unconscious psychological recesses of their mind. It was often a very painful process, but always rewarding. We learned a lot about ourselves personally and each other as a couple.

A Closer Look at Primal Fear

In our research, we learned how we were using psychological defenses to protect ourselves from feeling our childhood wounds. We used the term, "primal fear", to refer to the most distilled down core fear that we had. Through the process of looking within and questioning and asking why, with a lot of emotionality in between, we both finally came up with what our own primal fear was. What tumbled out of Barbara's mouth one Sunday afternoon was, "I feel invisible". What tumbled out of mine was, "I am afraid there is something wrong with me".

As a side note to Barbara's fear of being invisible, I want to mention that once we got into private practice and started learning what our client's primal fear was, one of the most common was that they felt invisible. And to illustrate that this particular primal fear is just as terrifying to someone that has it as any other primal fear, one of our clients, a female, who felt invisible, ended her life about a year after we closed our practice and moved to California.

What we learned about ourselves in relationship to Barbara's primal fear was this. I would do something like not fully listen to Barbara, and then have to ask her to repeat herself, and she would feel fearful inside. And, to the outside observer, if my not listening appeared to be at a pain level for Barbara of, say, two or three on a scale of one to ten, she would actually feel pain at the ten level. To Barbara, my not listening seemed to her as an attack on her by me. Her perception of attack was that I cared so little about her that I was intentionally ignoring her because she was unimportant to me and that my attention on myself, instead of her, was a hurtful, mean thing to "do" to her.

What Barbara's pain was really about was not having her needs met as a child by her parents, particularly her mother. Barbara was starved for attention as a child. And, as my example earlier about her and her older brother illustrated, her parents did nothing to keep her from being terrified and actually harmed by her older brother. She felt unlovable and unworthy and ultimately invisible, like she didn't even exist. In fact, she would often say, "I feel like I don't exist".

What we did with this pain of Barbara's was to take it into our relationship as "our" problem, "our" issue. We had made the decision, a long time before that, that we would see all problems in our relationship as "our" problem, as a couple problem, a relationship problem, that we would both work on to get resolved.

Prior to the time of our thesis research, we gave lip service to this decision. Now we fully knew that all of our problems were "our" problem and we proceeded in that manner. Of course, the first thing was that I had to value Barbara enough to really listen and hear her from then on. And that was easy because now I saw how absolutely important it was to Barbara for me to hear her in every respect, no matter what she was saying or talking about. That understanding about Barbara transformed me into an active, aware listener. It taught me how to listen. Barbara now had a partner, a loving supporter of hers that truly valued what she had to say and really listened to her.

Barbara's Inner Work

Barbara's work was to heal the false belief that she was invisible. She had to change her mind about herself and to do that she used two different levels of healing.

The first level was the purely psychological level. What she did there was to go back and do what we called "unwind" every false belief about her that was on top of, and contributed to, her believing that she was invisible or didn't exist. With us working together in a very loving, open and supportive way, she was able to identify key events and experiences in her childhood that caused her to believe she was not lovable enough to receive love and attention.

On top of that was the judgment of herself that she was not worthy of love and attention. Barbara had a very strong mind, exercised like an athlete in a gym, which was strong from her high degree of self-awareness and discernment and her ability to make decisions about herself and honor those decisions. So in a very typical one-fell-swoop fashion for Barbara, she was able to reinterpret those childhood experiences, and her beliefs about herself, into new beliefs that she was indeed not only worthy of love and attention but also lovable as a person. And from those two beliefs she then knew cognitively that she was visible and did exist.

The Ego

However, Barbara did not stop there. She knew that all of this primal fear was about the little self, or ego, that all humans make up in their minds. This is the ego in the purest spiritual definition of the term, not the ego of Freud or from any other psychological definition. In this sense, Barbara applied a purely spiritual approach to the ultimate healing of this false belief that produced primal fear within her mind. She knew that if she didn't do this, the purely psychological healing could unravel because she knew her ego, the original culprit that believed it was invisible, did not in fact exist and that it would eventually connect the terror of knowing that it did not really exist with the primal fear of being invisible and thus keep this mental construct alive in her mind.

The ego is nothing more than an idea of who we are that we make up in our minds and actually believe is us. At our deepest, real level of being, we unconsciously know that we are part of something much greater than a made-up self. We know we are part of one whole spirit and that the whole *is* every part. But the made-up self that we think we are does everything in its power to keep us from ever remembering that because, if and when we do, the part of our mind that believes in this little made-up self will be transformed into the original knowledge of who we really are and the ego will no longer exist.

So we, as the ego, are terrified of losing ourselves. If the ego goes away, we think we go away. The made-up self itself does know that it is just made-up and so is ultimately completely insecure and terrified for its "life". And that is where Barbara's fear of not existing came from. She figured this out and reached the point where she would say, "I, the little i, doesn't exist".

At first, she would still feel terror about that but instead of trying to hide and not feel that terror, she would become completely vulnerable and allow the terror while using her mind in the moment of terror, a holy instant, to continually uphold her belief that she was not only worthy of love, and lovable, but also that, at her core, her very essence, the spirit of her very being, was as God created her. It didn't take her long for the terror to diminish to merely being a feeling of discomfort and then it just went completely away, regardless of any stimulus to the contrary. Like a faded leaf being blown by a powerful wind, that old false belief just went away. Barbara had transformed her fear into love. It was a beautiful process to be a part of. As a result of the process, Barbara reached a whole new level of spiritual awareness. Our holy relationship had been a vehicle for spiritual transformation.

As mentioned earlier, Barbara did everything fast. That was because she had a tremendous value for not wasting time. And her leaving the physical at such an early age was a testament to that. I believe that at some level she always knew she was going to leave this lifetime earlier than expected. Barbara was no longer dancing the two-step tango. I was now dancing it all by myself.

The Two-Step Tango: My Version

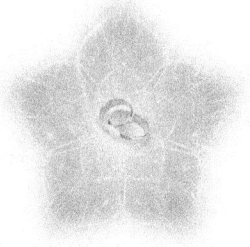

He has seen in another person the same interests as his own.[10]

—A Course in Miracles

The reason I was still dancing the two-step tango by myself is that I continued to hang on to my primal fear beyond the experience of our thesis research. I did learn a lot from our thesis research and I made major changes which I will share now.

What we learned about ourselves in relationship to my primal fear was this. We already knew that I had gone from being an ultra-responsible person back in my successful real estate broker days to having an aversion to responsibility after having destroyed my real estate company and allowed that experience to register in my mind that I not only failed, but that I *was* a failure. And that fit in perfectly with my primal fear that there was something wrong with me. In other words, I was a failure because there was something wrong with me.

By the time I began this thesis research, I had become a responsible partner to Barbara and a responsible professional business person again. However, in exploring the inner workings of my mind during the experiential thesis research, I realized that there was still a small part of me that was unconsciously giving my responsibility to Barbara. It played out in areas of our life like me giving responsibility to Barbara for the overall financial strategy of our lives. I executed, or was the tactician, of most everything we did, but Barbara was the strategist, the overall thinker and responsibility-taker of our relationship.

In not accepting full responsibility for everything in our relationship, and thus being a full co-leader of our lives, I was giving away part of my power to Barbara because, deep down and unconsciously, I didn't think I was good enough to take full responsibility. I was keeping the fear that there was something wrong with me alive by continuing, even in small, imperceptible ways, to have an aversion to full responsibility for myself and my life.

I was projecting my responsibility, for anything that I didn't want to be responsible for, onto Barbara. As a result, in those areas of responsibility I followed Barbara around like a puppy dog. And, in doing so, I created a prison for myself. I felt guilt and shame for not being fully present in our relationship in those areas of our relationship where I was projecting my responsibility onto her, and I blamed Barbara, and felt anger toward her, for anything relating to those responsibilities that I was unhappy about.

I lived in a self-created prison of guilt, shame and anger and it felt like Barbara was causing those emotions in me. It took a lot of internal digging, deep inner inquiry and introspection, to figure all this out about myself because these were mostly very subtle, non-surface things going on in our relationship, but between Barbara and I working on all of this, it all came out. When it all tumbled out, it looked ugly and abusive, but it felt like the weight of the world was now off my shoulders just by learning all of this about me.

I went to work immediately to take full responsibility for myself and my life. I looked at every nook and cranny of my life and made sure that I knew how I felt, what I really wanted, in all of those areas. Then I would collaborate with Barbara as partners on all of our decisions. Being the partner she was, Barbara had always encouraged me to know myself and to speak up about what I wanted. She herself had been a puppy dog following around her partners in previous relationships. But she changed all that before she met me.

By the time I met Barbara, she was a self-assured woman who knew what she wanted and took full responsibility for herself and her life. By the time of this thesis research, she had already taught me how she had worked her way out of not even knowing what she wanted to becoming self-aware enough to know what she wanted and to have the inner belief in herself to speak up to everyone about what she wanted. That previous teaching by Barbara, and learning by me, had gotten me to the current level of responsibility. With the thesis research, I was so angry at myself for discovering that I had still been hiding out in the more subtle areas of responsibility that I was determined to polish this off once and for all.

One Step Pain, Two Step Blame

This version of the two-step tango was me feeling pain from giving my responsibility to Barbara and projecting that pain onto Barbara as being her responsibility for my pain. One step, pain. Two step, blame. By the time we were out of graduate school and in private practice, I felt like I was so engaged in every aspect of our lives that I was truly taking responsibility for myself, my life and collaborating with Barbara as an equal partner about everything in our relationship. She told me when we moved to California that she felt like we were finally balanced.

Collaborate versus Compromise

By the way, I came up with the idea to use the word, "collaborate", instead of "compromise", in our relationship and Barbara agreed to it and we taught this to our clients once we became psychotherapists. Because of avoiding responsibility for so many years, it felt like I had compromised myself far too long and it felt so much better to make joint decisions as a couple on a collaborative basis. I saw this work well with our clients and I still believe in its use.

It is better for both partners to agree after collaborating on an issue than for one or both partners to compromise on a decision. And the secret to this is to look for what is best for the relationship. If something doesn't serve the relationship, then it can't serve both of the partners because ultimately the relationship will be in trouble. I believe a holy relationship always serves the best interests of both partners and, in doing so, also serves the best interest of the relationship itself.

Barbara and I were no longer projecting onto each other. We did have moments of feeling emotional pain that was stimulated by each other, but now we knew the pain was really coming from ourselves personally. It was easy for us at that point to trace down that emotional pain to something that was inside of us that was causing it and then change the false belief about ourselves that was causing it to something true and loving. This way, each person in the relationship gets to the very bottom of the cause of their emotional pain. From there, the fear is removed and love comes rushing in from where it always was: at the center of our being.

We were no longer doing the two-step tango. We felt like we were waltzing.

Judgment: The World's Prison

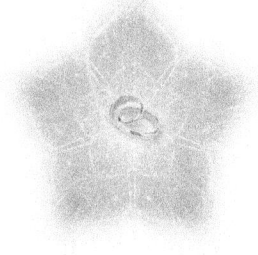

On Barbara's deathbed, when she was still able to speak, I asked her if there was anything she wanted to tell people at her funeral. I said it would be "no holds barred". Her reply was: "There's no use me preaching to people in arrears. There's so much judgment in the world, it doesn't need any from me."

We began writing our first book, *The Energy of Life*, as a way of clarifying for ourselves how life really works. We were using a synthesis of everything we had ever learned from ancient and contemporary Far Eastern and Western philosophy, religion, metaphysics and spirituality to come up with our own brand of spirituality. We knew we were walking our own unique path and we knew that a deluded person does not know s/he is deluded, so we were earnestly trying to uncover what was true and what was not about how the world works.

Judgment Always Separates

One morning, when we lived in the countryside outside of New Orleans, as we were walking our Weimaraner dog, Max, Barbara began to get insights about judgment and its role in how the world works. She began with the introductory idea that, "Judgment always separates". And from that one little idea we were off and running with a zeal for removing judgment from our consciousness and, thus, from our lives. We spent the next two decades working on how to do that. The work paid off.

In a holy relationship, there is really only joining, or union, or communion, or communication that is completely at one with itself, when two partners are both present in the holy instant. In that instant, it is literally like time stops because there is no past or future and birth of the new can take place. These moments, or instants, are truly rare because from the beginning of time we humans have trained ourselves to protect ourselves from a terrifying future by learning the lessons from the past. The only problem with that philosophy, or practice, or way of life, is that it doesn't allow for the full experience of what is, right now.

Down and Dirty, Quick and Easy

As humans, we basically have two "parts": one is real and the other is made up. The real part, or the real us, the real you, is the spirit that you are that animates your body. This spirit is literally the extension of the one source of everything into its, or Its, manifestation as creation. The spirit of God is creation. We *are* creation. But we believe we are some individual, separate thing that God created different, and separate from, Himself/Herself/Itself.

Right off the bat, there is a huge problem with this idea because, since the beginning of humans on the planet, we all, or mostly all, believe that God created the physical universe. From there you can add in the explanations held by every religion in the world, every aboriginal belief, and all the non-religious beliefs held by everyone else in the world, about why and how God made us, the Earth and why we are here.

We don't understand why God created sickness, war, pain, death and everything else that we don't like. And we pray to God to help us not have those things, except the death we believe is inevitable. And we believe that if we are a "good" person and don't do "wrong", we can have a happier life than otherwise and that we'll go to heaven when we die, if we believe in heaven. That's a down and dirty, quick and easy summary of the beginning of time to now, but there it is.

Ego versus Spirit

I've explained in Chapter One how we humans unconsciously believe that we have separated from our source, from God, and that the terror of this caused us to both make up a physical universe to project our belief in separation from source onto, and all the limitation that implies, complete with bodies to hide in, and to repress the whole thing never to be remembered again. We've done a great job of never remembering it again but fortunately there have been interventions into the collective consciousness of the human race to open us up to the truth about creation. The truth is we are one collective spirit, locked in the illusion that we are separate people, at the mercy of the health of our bodies, medical and physical science and race consciousness in general.

The second "part" of us humans is the part we made up in our minds, as I've described in Chapter One and thereafter. That's the ego or little self that we think we are. This part is an idea, or concept, of who we think we are that we hold, and protect dearly, at the very center of our conceptual mind.

Spirit, that we really are, is abstract and does not live

from and in concepts. This is the one Self that our source, God, created. The little self, that we made up conceptually, only lives from, and in, concepts. The Self experiences and the self conceptualizes. The former is real and the latter is fake.

Judgment: Right and Wrong, Good and Bad

From the beginning of the human race, we have conceptualized millions of years of being born, living and dying into the "right" way to *live* and the "good" way to *be* as a person. These millions of concepts are stored in the collective mind of race consciousness and are separated out in the doctrines and teachings and laws and way of life of all religions, governments, societies, cultures, families and groups of friends as *judgments* about how to live.

So what we have inside the human body is the underlying spirit of our source that has every attribute of God: love, intelligence, power, you name it. The energy of that spirit is what runs your body. If that energy, the very spirit of your being, were left alone to be and express exactly what it is, or Is, we would live the most miraculous lives imaginable, going in and out of our bodies at will and living under no laws but the one law, or reality, of creation. Your imagination can give you an idea of what that might be like.

On top of the underlying spirit that animates our bodies, or wrapped around it, are all of the concepts, the judgments, that we have taken in from race consciousness and use as our guide as how to live life. We use the very mind that we were given, the intelligence of spirit that we are, to continually live *from* and *as* mental conceptions of who and what we believe we are. We live as mental constructs or concepts based on the judgments we have about how to live.

Life versus Life-Time

Spirit experiences. The ego conceptualizes. The Self experiences. The self conceptualizes. Spirit, the Self, is eternal. The ego, the self, "dies" as a human because it identifies with the body and its frailty and because eventually all concept of self will be dissolved, or undone.

Now, if you have even $1/10^{th}$ of 1% of believability in what I'm saying, if you could feel even a little tiny bit of something inside of you resonating with what I've been explaining, which would be the real you coming through, how would you rather live: as life Itself or as a feeble representation of what life really is? Yes, I am saying that we *are* life because what God created *is* life. Life is the manifestation of Him/Her/It *as* life. What we are living here on Earth is a life-*time*. This lifetime will end with what we believe is "death". Life is eternal. The Self is eternal, the self is not.

The first paragraph of one of the beautiful lessons in *A Course in Miracles* says it perfectly: "There are not different kinds of life, for life is like the truth. It does not have degrees. It is the one condition in which all that God created share. Like all His Thoughts, it has no opposite. There is no death because what God created shares His Life. There is no death because an opposite of God does not exist. There is no death because the Father and the Son are one."[11]

Relationship as Vehicle to Awaken

Our work here on Earth is to awaken to the truth of who and what we really are. And holy relationships, with whomever, are the best vehicle to awaken us. They are the best vehicle for awakening because it is possible for two human beings to so connect with each other as to know their oneness and, in that oneness, awaken to the truth of oneness with all human beings and, ultimately, with our source, God, or whatever label you want to use for your source.

And this is why a holy relationship is sacred. And this is why I am writing this book. In a holy relationship, two people can trust each other so completely that all sense of needing to defend against future pain, based on past experience, can be let go so completely that the two partners merge into the experience of the presence of now and, in that presence, experience the oneness of being that they really are. Try that conceptually and you will find it to be impossible. Surrender fully to the present moment with your partner and you will discover something you may have never felt before. It can be peaceful, powerful, sensual, joyful, loving and any other label that could possibly describe the experience of being in the presence of *being*, without concept, *as* spirit, with another person.

In order to experience this, two partners in a holy relationship have to be without judgment about themselves and each other. That is because all judgment is judgment about ourself and, being painful, we project it out onto other people so that we can see them as "bad" and/or "wrong" and therefore not feel the emotional pain of our own self-judgment. We humans are judgment machines and our religions back us up on that. We believe God judges and that we have to be "good" and "right" to go to heaven.

Heaven and Hell

Here is what I have learned about that, from my experiences in the holy instant, and from the mystics of all religions. Heaven is spirit or Self. Hell is ego or self. God does not judge because God does not conceptualize. God is abstract and communicates in the language of the soul, or spirit, at a level of intelligence that is far beyond the conceptual imaginings of the little self, or ego.

We, as the ego, perceive or conceptualize everything. And the only things we perceive and conceptualize are extensions of our original false belief that we are separate from our source. We believe we are limited selves and, therefore, everything else we believe about how the world works, about how life is, about God, is limited. As spirit, we experience the truth of creation, not a symbol representing creation, in the form of words, beliefs, perceptions, mental constructs and judgments, but the actual experience of creation, of who and what we really are.

The good news is that we are literally using the intelligence of spirit that we are to make up the perceptions, beliefs, concepts and judgments of who and what we think we are. All that we are is always right here with us, as us, just waiting to be used as the expression of love that it really is. We have used our free will to make up a surrogate world for the non-physical creation that God created. We can experience the truth of creation right here on Earth in our holy relationships.

Our choice now is to live from experience by being fully present in each moment of life or to continue to "live" in a conceptual made-up world where we're continually trying each moment to figure out how to take care of the future based on our perceptions of the past. Let's consider how we might do that in the next two chapters.

Non-Judgment: Getting Out Of Prison – Barbara's Way

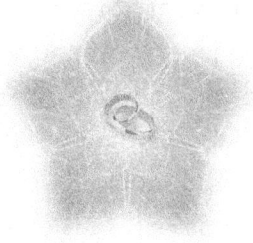

Wisdom is not judgment; it is the relinquishment of judgment.[12]
—A Course in Miracles

Barbara chose the perceptual way to finding the experience of the holy instant. I chose the experiential way. There is no right way or wrong way. There is only *your* way. I consider your way sacred and I'd like to explain why.

The Tao

Years ago I was fighting internally, within myself, about how to unconditionally love and accept myself. I wanted to know how to quit judging myself so that I could accept myself. So I went into a deep meditation and I ended up being taught something about The Tao, or The Tao Te Ching, that I had never understood before.

The Tao is an ancient Chinese spiritual text written sometime in the sixth century B. C. I used to read *about* The Tao from other sources during my first few years learning about, and practicing, metaphysics. When I worked in Manhattan and lived in Westchester County north of the city, I had a lot of time after work to ramble around by myself before I decided to catch a train home. On one of those evenings in a bookstore I decided to buy a copy of The Tao. I loved reading and studying it because it made me feel so free inside. It was often hard to understand, and puzzling, but I always got something out of it when I worked with it. So The Tao was already an old friend of mine that day that I went deep within myself to learn how to unconditionally love and accept myself.

I already knew that The Tao means, "The Way", as in the way to spiritual truth. What I learned in that meditative experience is that *the* way is *my* way. When I received that, it resonated with me immediately as truth and my heart felt like it broke wide open. The teaching was that, in this world of illusion, there is no *right* way of being or of living, only *your* way.

The reason your way is the way to live is because the you that you think you are is made up of countless choices and decisions you have made about yourself. Add to that the countless number of lifetimes that you have come here to incrementally learn the truth about who and what you are, and what you have is a complex set of beliefs about yourself that only you can unravel or unwind. There is no one way, or right way, to do that. There is only your way.

It is the part of your mind that believes you are the little self that you made up that needs to be transformed into the truth of who and what you are. That is a sacred path back home. And only you know the way back. Deep within yourself is the truth of who and what you are. Your life experiences give you the "friction", or pain, that you need to change your mind about yourself. If you use someone else's way, or path, back to your real home, you'll end up at their home and you'll have to eventually unwind that overlay onto your consciousness before you can get to the real work of unwinding your own false beliefs about yourself.

The Original Sin

As I said earlier, Barbara was the master of her mind. And she used it actively to create what she wanted in life. So it was natural and easy for Barbara to approach the holy instant from a perceptual standpoint. For those of

Getting Out of Prison - Barbara's Way   97

you with that same proclivity, I will share with you how Barbara did it so that you might apply it to yourself as an avenue into the holy instant. For those of you not used to using your mind to create consciously, these will be good lessons for you to use to begin to do so if you so choose.

It is one thing to have thoughts, perceptions, beliefs and judgments based on the past and projected into the future. That guarantees you a life based on your original perception that you are the little self that you made up in your mind, your ego that you think you are. From that perception, which in metaphysics is often considered the "original sin", comes thousands, millions, countless other perceptions based on that one original perception. That is how you have set up the part of your mind that thinks it is the ego. Nothing can come from the ego except what is like, or *of*, the ego.

Can you imagine what it must be like for that part of you, way deep down hiding inside of you, which believes that it actually left God, that it separated itself from your original source? Do you see how utterly terrifying that is? And how terrifying the consequent belief is that you caused the one creation of God, the Son of God, to be split into a million, or countless, pieces or parts, all autonomous and now separate instead of the original whole creation that your mind really knows it is part of? We have used the Christ mind that we really are to make up an ego mind that we are not. Do you see how utterly lost and terrifying that is to all of us?

It's all hidden deep inside, never to be discovered again, so that we'll never feel that terror. We also believe that if we don't remember that we separated from God, and have truly hidden that somewhere in the deep recesses of our mind, that God will never find us and we'll be safe from being punished by Him for leaving him and destroying his Son. Have you ever seen how a dog turns away from its owner when s/he doesn't want the owner to know s/he has done something the owner doesn't like? By turning away from the owner, the dog doesn't see the owner and thinks if s/he can't see the owner then the owner can't see her or him. That's exactly what we are doing in our hiding our original "sin" from God. In psychology, this is known as repression, which is unconsciously forgetting something because the feeling of the emotion behind the trauma we are hiding within ourselves is unbearable. It is also known as denial and this is the original denial that we all have made. We don't remember it, so we believe it doesn't exist. We deny it is there, so we believe it doesn't exist.

The Aversion to Truth

If you believe something doesn't exit, what is your response to anyone, or any idea, that is the opposite of what you believe? You will feel something like an aversion to what the person is saying, or to the idea you are reading. And if it's forced on you, it can feel like a life or death

Getting Out of Prison - Barbara's Way 99

situation because, to the ego, the false self that you made up, it *is* a life or death situation.

Everything in your mind comes from one or two sources: your real mind created by your real source or your made-up self made up by you. Every thought, every perception and every belief you ever have emanates from one of those two sources. So if you are faced with an idea that can literally unravel the lifetimes of belief that you are the little self that you believe you made up, you will defend against that idea unless and until you have finally experienced enough friction from life that an intervention has been created in your mind so that your mind is now receptive to the truth of who and what you are. It is my sincerest prayer that you have already had such an intervention or that these words *are* your intervention. Here is what *A Course in Miracles* says about this:

> *An imprisoned will engenders a situation which, in the extreme, becomes altogether intolerable. Tolerance for pain may be high, but it is not without limit. Eventually everyone begins to recognize, however dimly, that there must be a better way. As this recognition becomes more firmly established, it becomes a turning-point. This ultimately reawakens spiritual vision, simultaneously*

> *weakening the investment in physical sight.*
> *The alternating investment in the two*
> *levels of perception is usually experienced as*
> *conflict, which can become very acute. But the*
> *outcome is as certain as God.*[13]

The Ego's Defense System

So with this false self, the ego, that we have made up in our mind, we have made up everything about the world and how it works, all based on the limitations of what the ego really is. The ego is not real so nothing in the physical universe is real in that it all eventually turns back into the original energy, the raw intelligence of Divine mind, from which it is made. Mountains, planets, suns, bodies, all of it, all revert to the nothingness that it really is. And from this lack of permanence, we have made up science to prove to ourselves how everything works so that we can create some kind of protection for ourselves by living within the boundaries of science. However, no matter how many Ph.D.'s we have, or how exclusively we eat and drink only "healthy" foods, or how "right" we are or how "good" we are, our bodies eventually "die". But we have countless perceptions, concepts, beliefs and judgments about how to live so we can live as long as possible, and as healthy as possible. This is the defense system of our ego.

And this entire belief system is based on a very fragile,

made-up false self that is constantly trying to figure out how to continue existing in a limited world it sees of lack, uncertainty and death.

With those kinds of perceptions, no one will ever enter a holy instant.

Barbara's Way

Barbara knew all of this and began basing all of her perceptions on the truth that she was learning, and the guidance she was getting, in meditation. She was taught that if her mind contained only perceptions of truth that she would create the necessary conditions within her mind to be able to experience the holy instant.

As I have explained, we always perceive from either our Christ mind or our ego, from Self or from self. The ego will never allow us to have only perceptions of truth. It may convince us that all of our perceptions are of truth, but those perceptions will be egoic perceptions disguised as truth. It is very easy for our ego to disguise itself as a wolf in sheep's clothing. So it takes vigilant discernment, total in-the-moment awareness, to know that we are perceiving only truth. This is the path that Barbara chose to the holy instant in order to be able to live in non-judgment.

Financial and Time Freedom

We left our practice of psychotherapy, and moved to

the mountains of Northern California, in order to devote our time and attention to the learning and living of truth. Our first year here provided the environment for us to relax and let go of a lifetime of chasing money and freedom. We had consciously worked for years to create a life of "financial and time freedom", to quote the decision we made that was embodied in our united affirmation and visualization. Now we were actively living our creation and our meditations got deeper and deeper.

One year after arriving in California Barbara was diagnosed with uterine cancer. After a successful surgery and a reduced version of the recommended dose of chemotherapy, every test showed that Barbara was cancer free. We believed that was the case, but we lived with the keen sense of not knowing how much more time we had together.

All of her life, Barbara lived with a sense of immediacy about the time she had available to her. She directed her time, consciously, so that she was always creating the life she wanted. After the intervention of the cancer diagnosis, surgery and chemotherapy, Barbara lived in an almost continuous stillness that had previously been unknown to her. Her quiet time and meditations were longer and deeper and became integrated into her being in such a way that her peace, joy and love were always palpable to me. All distractions from the outside world now became minor and insignificant, no matter what they were. And the harmony between us became like a symphony, an easy moving, never-ending symphony of connectedness and mutual support.

During this time, we no longer needed the other to mirror to us our judgments because they all just melted away. We lived largely in seclusion, like we were in an ongoing retreat for two, happily ensconced in our beautiful home that was surrounded by nature. So we didn't have much stimulus from the outside world to potentially activate judgment from us about anyone or anything outside of ourselves. We also had a clear and firm understanding, and appreciation, that any and all judgment that we ever had about the other was really about ourselves.

For the first time in our 22 years together, we were able to easily see and accept any and all judgments that we might project onto the other as judgments that were really about ourselves. And since we had discovered, so many years before in the writing of our book, *The Energy of Life*, that judgment was anathema to our soul, we began dropping judgment after judgment from our mind and loving and accepting ourselves as we were. All of the little bitty hidden judgments that we had managed to hide away from ourselves, even after all of our years of consciously working for self-awareness, and applying psychospiritual therapy to ourselves, came to the surface and simultaneously began falling away and being replaced by unconditional love and acceptance of ourselves.

Barbara's version of all of this was to consciously choose, actually decide, *against* self-judgment and *for* unconditional love and acceptance of herself. And in her powerful and masterful fashion, she did just that. From there, the doorway was wide open for her to consciously work her way into deciding to live in truth instead of illusion, in the Christ mind instead of ego, in love instead of fear. These were the necessary conditions that facilitated her living in the holy instant.

Barbara chose the holy instant, she decided for the holy instant, because she believed that only love was real. She lived *from* and *in* that belief. That belief occupied most every moment of Barbara's life. At that time in Barbara's life, there was no room for the past or the future. In those conditions she was able to experience the holy instant. And without the past or the future, there is only "what is" which is the very basis of non-judgment.

Love versus Fear

Although we can easily disguise fear as love in our minds, like when we disguise "taking" as "giving" and it "feels" like love, it is, nevertheless, relatively easy to know the difference between love and fear, especially if you enter into an exploration of both. It can be, however, much harder to know if we are living in and from truth or in and from illusion, if we are in the Christ mind or in our ego. Barbara was a master at knowing the real difference between love and fear. She could spot fake love a mile off, especially if it was me doing it. And she could spot it in herself instantly and sweep it right out of her mind. Her inner work now took on the "earnestness of love".[14]

Love became Barbara's radar, her sonar, her gyroscope, as she actively decided to transform all perceptions in her mind from fear to love. She knew that the essence of the Christ mind was love and that the essence of ego was fear. She also knew that even though pure truth can only be experienced in the abstract, that the perception of truth could lead her to the doorway of truth. And that is where she wanted to be.

What is Truth?

When I use the term, "truth", I am referring to what God, our source, created: nothing more, but also nothing less. There really *is* nothing more and there really *is* nothing less.

Truth is the reality of what God created. Nothing else exists. Nothing else can exist except as an expression of its source. And there is only one source. Creation can be seen, then, as the extension of our source into the manifestation of itself, or Itself. That manifestation is who and what we are.

The self we believe we are is an illusion we made up in

our minds. It is a manifestation of our minds into a belief of who and what we are. We believe we are something we are not. But how do we access *who* we really are, *what* we really are? Since we are wrapped up in believing we are something that we are not, the little self or ego, the roadmap back to who and what we really are is found in the learning of who and what we are *not*.

This is very similar to the process I have heard that Michelangelo used in his sculpture. He could see what was in the stone and sculpted away what was not part of it. In so doing, he was freeing what he saw in the stone from the stone. That is at least a good analogy of what is going on here. It's like our ego, or we ourselves as our ego, has us stuck in stone and thinking we are the stone. The ego is really the stone and who and what we really are needs to be freed from the stone, from the grip of the ego, by identifying what the ego is.

When we can see the ego for what it is, we can begin the process of deciding for its opposite. I say "begin" because even though it is simple once we see the ego for what it is, the process itself is hard because we have lifetimes of conditioning, full of countless ideas and beliefs, that we are our ego. And that conditioning, and its underlying energetic equivalent, feels to us like an aversion, a very strong one, the strongest one possible, as we begin to recognize our ego for what it is and to choose differently as we decide for the truth of who and what we really are.

The Path of Love

Barbara knew we cannot find our real selves through the ego. The ego only sees manifestations of itself. It can never see anything else. However, our real mind is forever connected to, and a part of, the mind of God. That is why it is often labeled the Christ mind. Since the essence of the Christ mind is love, and is always present in our mind, all it takes is for the love in our mind to be awakened and, at that moment, our path back home has begun.

Barbara's path back home had been awakened for a long time. She knew love. And she used her emotional gyroscope of love to identify when she was not in love, and/or the discernment of her mind to notice when she was choosing fear, and applied the power of her mind as a chisel, like Michelangelo, to remove beliefs about herself that she knew were fear-based and false. The removal process is a process of seeing fear in the light of love and, in so doing, the choice for love becomes obvious.

An Emotional Approach

Two approaches to this are very useful. The first, an emotional approach, is to use your emotional gyroscope of self-awareness to keep you in touch with whether you are in love or fear. With enough practice, you will develop a certainty about whether you are in love or fear. You will come to know what love feels like and what fear feels like.

I'm referring here to the more subtle forms of love and fear, rather than the more obvious ones. For example, if you see a snake and get afraid, you know you are in fear. If you see a newborn baby and feel a wonderful emotion inside, you know you are in love. Those types are obvious. But let's say you are "giving" to your child or partner, or your boss or friend. Are you really giving or are you actually trying to get something in return by your giving?

True giving is complete within itself and expects nothing in return. In fact, true giving is actually receiving simultaneously the energetic equivalent of what you're giving. Giving to get is taking in the disguise of giving. Giving is love. Taking is fear. For example, you are full of love after an afternoon in your flower garden and you want to share that love with your neighbor by bringing over flowers from your garden. That could easily be an example of love. On the other hand, you may not like your neighbor because her dog barks all the time and you want to bribe your neighbor with some flowers from your garden in the hopes that she will figure out a way to quiet her dog. That would be an example of trying to get something in the guise of giving, which is taking.

These are simple examples to illustrate the subtleties of love and fear. With practice, anyone can learn to know if they are in love or fear. When you're in love, you love and appreciate it. You enjoy it. And, because of its nature, when you're in love you always want to extend it, to give it away. Paradoxically, by giving it away you don't lose it. Rather, by extending it, by giving it away, you increase it within your consciousness because the act of giving is an inner affirmation that you *have* what you are giving. And the more we give love, the more we know that we *are* love. And once we know we are love, it will bubble up continuously and deliciously from within us and will naturally spill over to everyone and everything we experience. If we are full of love and it is overflowing within us, there is nothing left to do but to give it away.

Barbara knew there were only two emotions: love and fear. "Fear and love are the only emotions of which you are capable".[15] All other emotions emanate from those two. So an emotional gyroscope is a very useful tool to identify fear. It's a matter of asking yourself what are you afraid of if you are feeling any kind of emotion that is the opposite of love.

Love has many beautiful expressions, like joy, peace, beauty, harmony, serenity, connectedness, etc. Fear has many ugly expressions, like anger, guilt, shame, blame, defending, etc. Barbara and I often asked an angry client what they were afraid of and the answer was often an immediate and incredulous, "I'm not afraid". Of course, upon probing, we would help the client see what s/he was really afraid of. And that's what Barbara did during this process of identifying her false beliefs, or ego beliefs, and replacing them with beliefs that are rooted in truth.

A Mental Approach

The other approach to identifying and removing fear-based false beliefs about yourself is a cognitive, or mental, one. Your mind becomes the watcher, or witness, or observer of your thoughts. And your choice for love becomes your fulcrum for replacing fear-based false beliefs about yourself, and how the world works, with truth.

Barbara had many notes to herself about this process and she had a book in progress that she really wanted us to write called, *The Wiles of the Ego*. She felt like such a book would be very helpful to people by explaining what I am describing here. The wiles of the ego are the disguises of the ego. And Barbara went after them with a vengeance. Although I am not going to describe the various common disguises, or wiles, of the ego in this book, I do hope you are seeing that the essence of the ego is fear.

By going through this process, Barbara filled her mind with the perception of truth. Every time she noticed fear in her, she traced it down until she could find a thought or belief that was causing the fear. She then looked at that fear from the center of her being, from the truth of her Christ mind, and saw the fear as an impossibility in the light of who and what she knew she was.

She then let the fear go and replaced it with a conscious belief of the truth about herself and made a conscious decision to honor that truth. She did this time and again, over and over, until fear was removed from her consciousness, from her mind. The result was that the underlying love became ever present in Barbara's mind and she was happier, more joyful and more at peace, than at any time in her life.

The Absence of Fear

When the perceptions of the mind are only of love, are only of the truth of who and what we really are, there is nothing in the mind to produce fear. In the absence of fear, the mind relaxes and simply surrenders to what is. The mind is clear. The mind is certain of who and what it is. With clarity and certainty, all of the mind is now fully present in the moment. There is no defending against a fictitious future based on the fears of the past. There is no busyness going on in the mind because there is no reason for it. The conditions necessary for the holy instant, and therefore non-judgment, have been met.

Barbara reached this level of presence in her mind. She was truly living in the presence of being. And in that presence of being she truly experienced the holy instant. She was now experiencing life, fully present in each moment, free of judgment and no longer following conceptual ideas of *how* to be; instead, she was just *being*.

Non-Judgment: Getting Out Of Prison – My Way

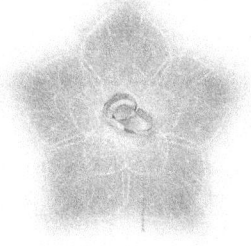

The holy instant is a time in which you receive and give perfect communication. This means, however, that it is a time in which your mind is open, both to receive and give. It is the recognition that all minds are in communication. It therefore seeks to change nothing, but merely to accept everything.[16]

—A Course in Miracles

I chose the experiential way to finding the experience of the holy instant. I will explain how I got there in the hope that it will help you to learn to surrender to, and trust, the holy instant. My experience with it has truly been life-changing. It is what finally allowed me to start living truth instead of just paying lip-service to it. The following is a summary of my path to the holy instant.

An Intervention Into Consciousness

On the Saturday before my birthday, November 19th, 1988, Barbara and I had another experience with MDMA. Since our May of 1988 experience on that beach in Hawaii, I had been working at a much higher level of desire to live in truth. I had tasted truth, pure expansive love, on that beach and I wanted so much to live it. However, I still had a lot of fear in my consciousness and I felt stuck in it. That Saturday afternoon in 1988 served as an intervention into my consciousness that caused a permanent change onto the path of love.

I did not know in advance the transformative power of MDMA those two times that I experienced it. Each were unique and the second more powerful than the first. It has served as an intervention that I needed to release fear and open to love that I could integrate within me on a permanent basis. By sharing these experiences with you, it is my belief that you can create your own intervention because you now have the believability of their possibility. MDMA did not *give* me a permanent change in my consciousness. It gave me the believability that those changes were possible. It is my *living* the possibilities that created the reality of them. I believe that your knowing of the possibilities, and my explanation of how to experience them, is all the stimulus you need to create them for yourself.

We were advised this time, by our psychiatrist and psychotherapist friends, to use dosages that were more appropriate to our respective body metabolisms. Because of that, I used a little more and Barbara used a little less. The result was that I experienced a complete release of fear from my consciousness. It was truly the most amazing experience of my whole life. My body began shaking and I simultaneously experienced fear-based ideas and beliefs pouring out of my mind, and the corresponding emotion of fear in my body being released, all at once over about a 30 minute time span. It felt like peals of thunderclouds being removed from my mind and body. I had fear after fear after fear leave my mind and pass through and out of my body and, amazingly, I also experienced the love that was encasing, and surrounding, all of the fear that I felt leaving me. When it was over, I literally felt like a new person. I felt lighter and freer and my mind was completely and utterly clear, crystal clear.

The next morning I expected the fear to return, but it didn't. I felt a little groggy from the drug, but still wide open and free, with a crystal clear mind. And the whole day went that way. The following morning, a Monday, I was rested and felt wonderful and my mind was still crystal clear. I was concerned that if a fear came up, I would defend against it and all the fear would come rushing back. That concern produced a tinge of fear but I just allowed it to pass through my mind and body and my total openness and crystal clear mind remained. I was elated.

Walking down the stairs to join Barbara for breakfast, I knew something fundamental had changed as I heard Bryant Gumbel's voice coming from the Today Show on television. Hearing his voice, I felt an intense and all-encompassing interest in every word he was saying. It was unlike anything I had ever felt before. I was alive and on fire with interest in life without a scintilla of self-focus. I was fully present, totally encapsulated in the holy instant.

This continued for two full weeks. Since knowing Barbara, I had been amazed at how in-the-moment and clear her mind always seemed to be. But now she, and another friend of ours, both commented to me, at different times, how they wished their mind was as crystal clear as mine. They could sense the stillness and presence of mind that I had and were mirroring back to me how wonderful that was.

These are the other things that happened as a result of that experience. During those two weeks I never consciously thought of anything, ever. I was simply fully present in the moment and lived within, and from, that. I knew what to do, and what to say, at all times. And there were three other amazing things that I experienced during those blissful two weeks in 1988.

First, I never had to try to remember anything. If I needed to remember something, it was just there, right there in my mind. If I wanted to reference something from the past, or if Barbara asked me something about the past, it was just there, right there in my mind, without even the slightest bit of conscious mental effort on my part at all.

That has been, and still is, my standard for memory. If it serves me to remember something, it is right there. If it doesn't come, then it obviously is a waste of time and is not needed because it was an ego urge to remember the past.

The second and third things were in combination with each other. I never went back to the past and I never analyzed anything. I lived fully present in the here and now and I just intuited, or knew, whatever I needed to know. It was like non-thinking but knowing the results of what thinking could produce. I felt totally free and alive during this entire two week period.

As a student of metaphysics, I have long since not believed in accidents or coincidences. I have known that every effect has a cause, whether the cause is obvious or not. And I've had a deep appreciation for the connectedness of everything in the universe. With that in mind, I will share with you that a lifelong friend of mine had the exact same experience as I did during those same two weeks of November, 1988, and we didn't even learn about each other having the same experience until about 15 years later. These respective interventions were major events in both of our lives and were, I believe, part of the overall causative factors that have facilitated both of us to now have a great respect for the present moment and living in the now.

What I Learned

Fear did return, after those two weeks, in both my friend and I. But I had a profound learning experience that changed my consciousness and that eventually helped me to return to living in the present and, thus, the holy instant. Here is what I learned:

I learned that I don't ever have to be concerned about memory. It takes care of itself.

I learned that not only do I not need to hang on to the past, or project into the future, but that doing so takes me out of the present moment.

I learned that my full power is present in the fullness of each moment.

I learned that my full intelligence is present in the fullness of each moment.

I learned that I am highly intuitive in the fullness of the present moment and that I can trust my intuition explicitly.

I learned that fear cannot live in the fullness of the present moment and that only love does.

I learned that I can trust the fullness of the present moment and that whatever I need in the present moment is always there.

I learned that I don't need armor from the past to protect me from a fearful future.

I learned that the past is over and the future doesn't exist.

I learned to trust myself, and life, in the fullness of the present moment.

The Fullness of the Present Moment

I lived in and out of the present moment for over a decade. When I was out of the moment, it was because I allowed some outside stimulus from the challenges of life, usually about work, money, my body or my relationship with Barbara, to scare me out of the present moment. In 2001 I became completely overwhelmed by one of our many moves into a new house (when Barbara finished decorating a house the Gemini in her was ready to move) and the intense stock trading I was doing. I noticed the fear and stopped everything. I sat down, took a few deep breaths and went into a deep meditation. The inspiration I got in that meditation was, "In the present moment, you always have all the time you need for everything". That resonated so deeply within me that I knew it was truth.

In other words, the fullness of the moment takes care of itself. There is never regret (the past) in the present moment. There is never anticipation (the future) in the present moment. And because the present moment is full of itself, there is never any thought or concern about anything except the present moment.

From that moment on, I have unequivocally believed in and trusted the present moment. That inspiration is a continual mantra for me.

Knowing From the Heart

In June of 2005 I was hurrying to my car to go teach a psychology course and I was concerned with being late because of the traffic. I had a check in my hand that I was going to deposit for Barbara's mother after class. I mindlessly (out of the moment because of being in a hurry) put the check on top of the car as I loaded my briefcase and breakfast into the car. On the freeway I realized that I forgot to get the check off the top of my car. I began to panic but instantly realized there was nothing I could do about it then and consciously decided to become fully present in the moment. I put on inspirational music and began communing with spirit. I was fully present and therefore had no concern whatsoever about the check. I knew it would work out.

While communing with spirit, or the Christ mind within, I received guidance on how to expand the course material for the day into a broader, more truth-based version of why and how the material would help my students in their lives. I often made notes while driving, but knew that I didn't need to this time. As I walked down the hallway toward my classroom door I could feel in my heart that I would know what to say, and how to say it, in the present moment. For the first time, my sense of the present moment came from my heart and I had the intuition that the heart is how we feel our soul, or spirit. From that moment on, my heart, or heart center, or heart chakra, became my connection to a felt sense of me as spirit. That felt sense has never left me. It is how I know I am fully present in the moment.

My class that day was a wonderful experience of connection with my students. It was like I experienced the class instead of taught it. And that's how it was from then on.

Seeing with Vision

On the way home, I thought about the check that was no longer on top of my car. As I turned off the freeway I had a felt sense that the check was under a tree by our house. I could even see the check under the tree. When I got to the block where we lived, I drove very slowly and noticed a tree on the right just a few feet from the corner. As I drove by I didn't see the check. But instead of continuing to drive and keep looking, I could sense that it was there so I pulled over to the curb, got out of the car and walked back toward the tree. There under the tree was the check, except that it was torn up into little pieces and put in a pile. It was like someone found it and, to prevent anyone from taking it and trying to cash it, they tore it up for me. I had had many intuitive experiences before that, but that was my first ever psychic experience where I could actually see something in my mind's eye that solved a problem for me. With that experience, and the teaching one just before, I became more convinced than ever of the value of living in the present moment.

The Power of Now

I also have to give credit to Eckhart Tolle for the influence his work, and his book, *The Power of Now*, has had on me being able to live in the present moment. I read the book in early 2005 when I was working on my graduate thesis, but I didn't actually work with, or use, the ideas from the book. I was completely inspired by the book, but I must not have been ready for it yet because I didn't use the book to help me be in the present moment. But on May 23, 2005, Barbara's birthday, she gave me a copy of a much smaller version of Tolle's work called, *Practicing the Power of Now*. That book, in conjunction with *A Course in Miracles*, changed my life forever.

By the way, from that first trip to Hawaii on Barbara's birthday back in 1988, Barbara always gave me a present on her birthday. That was just her loving way and she called it a celebration of life for both of us. Of course I received the underlying gift of giving and also gave a gift to Barbara on my birthday from then on.

After my experience with the lost check on top of the car, and my renewed interest in being fully present in the moment, I went to the part of A Course in Miracles devoted to the holy instant. I began studying and practicing the ideas there on a daily basis and also taking them deep into meditation on a regular basis.

Right after that, I received *Practicing The Power of Now* from Barbara and began using it to help me live in the present moment. I can truly say that my first experience of intentionally sinking deep down into presence, or the presence of being, was as I practiced the lessons from *Practicing The Power of Now*. That book has always felt like a how-to book to help me live in the holy instant as explained in A Course in Miracles. I use *Practicing The Power of Now* to this day. It is on my night table right now. The way I use it is to only read one small section at a time and then apply that section for a day or many days. And I keep doing that until I finish the book. Then I'll put it down until I sense that I can use a refresher. I almost know the book by heart now so I don't read it as much as I used to, but I still use it as a primer for living in presence whenever I feel the need. I did just finish it again a couple of months ago and I just re-read the section on relationships a few weeks ago. So I endorse *Practicing The Power of Now* wholeheartedly. I've also done the same with Tolle's other two inspirational books, *Stillness Speaks* and *Oneness With All Life*. Thank you, Eckhart Tolle.

I want to say that my path to the holy instant has been a long one. I never could get there until I began having the experiences I have just described. Before those experiences, I was a very high strung, intense Scorpio energy with countless things on my mind that I reacted to from moment to moment in a frenetic and fearful way. As I've described in Chapter Three, when I destroyed my real estate company I became obsessive, fearfully worrying about things over and over. And I tried to master my mind over and over but never could. It was only with the experiences that I've described, and the value and respect that I had for living in the moment, that I finally arrived there.

That is not to say that everybody has to use MDMA, or experience the kind of pain I have, in order to live in presence. I have, in fact, met one person, a beautifully vibrant and alive young woman, the year I lived in Manhattan that had a crystal clear mind and it just seemed so natural for her to be that way, without needing pain or drugs to get her there. And I've seen others into whose eyes I have gazed that seemed to have a crystal clear mind.

Another such person was a woman I met on the subway in Manhattan. We were hanging onto the same pole in the middle of the subway car and I noticed she was reading a spiritually-based book of the type that I was always reading so I engaged her in conversation. She looked up from the book and had the same clear eyes as the young woman I've described just above. I wanted so much to get to know this person, to engage her, to learn from her, to share with her, so at the end of the ride I asked her if we could have coffee right then. She looked me right in the eyes with the deepest gaze and said, "I can't do that. I'm afraid it would distract me from my path." I told her I respected that and we parted with a smile.

I believe anyone with the full intention to live in the presence of being in the holy instant will attract and/or create the conditions necessary for that experience. It is the fear of loss, based on the false beliefs of the ego, which prevents us from living in the fullness of the here and now. That is why I offer these experiences to you, so that you might join with Barbara and me in knowing the value of the holy instant. And, with that value, a new treasure of your heart, you can more easily let go of the ego and fear and fall into the fullness of the holy instant and love.

Your Way

I cannot say that my method of arrival into the holy instant is better than Barbara's or that hers was better than mine. But I do think that somewhere between the two methods lies your way into the holy instant. It is my sincerest prayer that you have already found your way into the holy instant or that you are now on your way to arriving there.

Since my experience in Manhattan with the two naturally in-the-moment women, I have met many other people who seem to naturally live most of their moments in presence. And I have now had the experience of allowing myself to use the power of my mind to not only be fully present in the moment but also to make self-loving and self-responsible choices for myself in the moment. I now know that non-judgment, or to say it in reverse, unconditional love and acceptance, reside in the holy instant.

In conclusion, I would say that if you are like me and have a wild, unruly mind, then my approach to the present moment will probably serve you best. Once you have mastered your mind enough to be able to be present in the here and now, you can then integrate the mastery of your mind with conscious decisions and choices that come from self-love and self-responsibility and can begin to create from desire as Barbara did. On the other hand, if you already master your mind more than it masters you, you can use a perceptual approach to the holy instant and to non-judgment similar to Barbara's.

Special Relationships

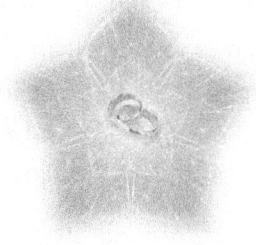

God created the only relationship that has meaning, and that is His relationship with you.[17]

—A Course in Miracles

Before we go any further in the exploration of holy relationships, I believe it is a good time to consider special relationships. Special relationships are the most common relationships. They are what we usually start with. They are the relationships that the human race has had from the beginning of time. A special relationship is what Barbara and I had the whole time we were working so hard to create a holy relationship.

Special relationships are based on fear. We *unconsciously* design them to facilitate the continuation of the little self that we believe we are in this world. Holy relationships are based on love. We *consciously* create them as a way to learn the truth of ourselves as the Self created by our source, or God.

Let's consider how and why special relationships are based on fear.

A Fragile Idea

As we come into a lifetime to have experiences that will ultimately get us closer to the realization of knowing who and what we really are, we still come in to human form with the unconscious core belief that we are separate from our source. Most everybody on the planet believes the same thing and we all see the world as limited, as a place of challenge in order to survive, much less thrive. We do "tame" the world in our minds, so to speak, as we develop our unique talents and learn and grow and develop what feels like satisfying and supporting relationships. Many of us see the world as beautiful and life as a gift. But under all of that is still the unconscious belief that we are separate from our source and the emotion of that is fear.

Remember that we made up this physical universe, including the planet Earth, and our bodies, as a way to hide ourselves in physical form both from God and from ever remembering the primal terror of believing we left our source, and, in doing so, destroyed His creation, His one Son, which is us, our one Self. At our deepest level of unconscious fear we believe we are individual selves, yet, at our deepest core level, where love resides, we know we are one Self, the Self of creation. This disconnection in our consciousness causes us to believe we have in fact somehow destroyed God's creation, His Son.

So, by definition, from the standpoint of our separated minds that made up the physical universe, everything about Earth is limited. It is limited because we made the physical universe, and all physical form including our bodies, out of the original fragile idea that we are who we made up in our minds. Underneath that fragile idea we are hiding the truth of who and what we are from ourselves, but deep down inside of our mind we know that we are as God created us. The truth of who and what we are has never changed and cannot be changed. What God created will always be. So we are connected to the one Christ mind that we all are, and we know it at the deepest level of ourselves, yet we're using a part of our Divine mind to believe that we are a fragile, limited being in an ever-changing world.

Do you see how terrifying to us that really is? We know we are something that we are acting like we are not. Do you see how unstable that little self we believe we are must be? And, from all of that, can you see how the whole thing we have constructed in physical form is but a limited representation of who and what we really are? We have made up in our minds a limited planet, with limited resources that everyone is competing for in one way or the other. Because of this, we make up strategies for ourselves as to how best to live in the world. The cave man and woman, our first version of ourselves (not a very good job, was it?), formed the first strategies for how to survive in this world and that has been passed on and improved on for millennia. And one of the primary strategies for surviving in this world is the special relationship.

Appearances

If we were using all of our mind, and therefore just our Christ mind, we would see all human beings as different aspects of one connected energy. We would innately know the oneness that we are with everyone and everything. In oneness, no one is special because we're all the same. The *appearance* of each of us as being different is simply a reflection of the various personalities that our little self has made up, but underneath that we are all the same.

Pick the most extreme idea about the power of God from whatever religious tradition you most believe in and apply that to the idea of humans being created different for whatever reason you believe in. You would probably use a term like, "omniscient", or "omnipresent" or a similar term or idea for the power of God, representing the idea that God is everywhere and everything. And, if that's so, if we are created *by* God, and therefore *from* God, how could God be everywhere and everything but humans *be* different? And how could the physical universe, as vast and amazing as it is, be something so that every part of it eventually deconstructs or dissolves back into the original non-form from which it started? The answer is, only if it is not real, which it isn't. Our little self made it up. But the essence of everyone and everything is the one light of creation as expressed by our source.

Holy relationships are vehicles for two people to realize their oneness, fully extend themselves to each other, and, in the fullness of that love, extend themselves to everyone and everything as part of who and what they are. They are primary facilitators for us learning who and what we really are.

Cave Man and Woman Model

Special relationships are vehicles to defend against who and what we are. We unconsciously use them as a way to continue our illusion that we are separate from our source. We see ourselves as separate beings, separate from everyone and everything. That alone is a terrifying perspective of ourself and the world. So we use the cave man and woman model and form tribes, or families and extended families of like-minded people for the purpose of helping each other survive and thrive in the world we see. And at the core of all tribal connections is the special relationship. The most common type of special relationships are, of course, life partners. But all other relationships are also special. Just think of every type of relationship you have in your life and those are the examples I am referring to.

A Very Special, Special Relationship

I used to think, for example, that the relationship with my maternal grandmother was the most wonderful and beautiful one in my life, prior to meeting Barbara. And Barbara thought the same thing about her relationship with her father. When both of these special people in our respective lives left the physical at about the same time, right after Barbara and I got together as a couple, it convinced us even more than ever that the unconditional love and acceptance of those two loving people was replaced by our own unconditional love and acceptance of each other. We thought our holy relationship had now taken the place of those other two holy relationships. But as the friction of our relationship with each other began to occur, we began to realize we weren't in a holy relationship. And, with therapy, introspection and insight from meditation, we both learned that Barbara's relationship with her father, and mine with my grandmother, were not as perfect as we had thought.

What was brought to my attention in meditation was how I was trained, by my grandmother, to be fundamentally influenced to always have to be "good" and "right", and all variations thereof, based on her religious beliefs and the way she believed the world worked. So, by definition, if there was a "good", there had to be a "bad", and if there was a "right", there had to be a "wrong". And that's the very essence of judgment: the separating of good from bad and right from wrong.

The result was that all of my relationships, starting with my relationship with myself, had to be based on the foundational value of everyone being a "good" person that always did what was "right". And, without actually using the label of "special", all of my relationships, of all kinds, were special relationships. I was conditioned, trained if you will, to always be good and right and to seek out and form relationships only with people who were also good and right. All other people, that were "bad" and "wrong", were in another special category of not being appropriate for me to be in relationship with.

I still love my grandmother, by the way. And Barbara always loved her father. They were just our modern versions of how to live in a tribe, or in special relationships, no different than Barbara and I were with ourselves.

There are countless versions of what I have just described. There are countless types of special relationships, all based on how we see ourselves and the world. The following is Barbara's version based on her conditioning, or training, from her father.

Another Very Special, Special Relationship

Although a wonderful and loving man, as described in Chapter Two, Barbara's father was highly co-dependent on Barbara's mother, his wife, for his own self-acceptance and self-esteem. And that is basically the definition of co-dependence: having the inner need for outside approval by other people in order to feel good about yourself.

So Barbara was conditioned, trained, by her father, just from her experiencing his way of being in the world, to also be co-dependent. Specifically, she experienced, time and again, her father choosing her mother over her when many times she knew in her heart that she deserved the love she was asking for from him but was denied by him as he chose Barbara's mother's decisions over Barbara's needs.

This is not to say that Barbara's mother was "wrong" or "bad", and neither was her father. However, Barbara lived from a wide-open heart all of her life and she could feel, especially as all children do, when love resonated with her and when it was denied. She did receive unconditional love and acceptance from her father as she followed him around as a child being his helper on Saturday's during his chores around the house. Love flowed both ways then and Barbara could feel it.

With Barbara's mother, she had to earn her love, so to speak, by following the dictates of her mother. This was her mother's way, the way her mother was conditioned, was trained. So Barbara left her family life as a young adult being well conditioned into co-dependence. This played out as a strong need to achieve as she exhibited excellence in everything she did as her way of earning love and respect from other people and the world in general. Her relationships were special as she sought out relationships and situations where she could excel and earn other people's admiration and respect.

I came to Barbara at a time in my life when I needed, or, more truthfully, wanted, someone to take care of me. That matched perfectly with Barbara's need to excel as a wife and partner and, in taking care of me, helping me to patch up my broken wings and learn to fly again. She did an extraordinary job. I, on the other hand, performed perfectly in my duties as a loyal husband and partner so that I could be a "good" person doing everything "right". Her co-dependence and my dependence fit like a glove.

We felt like we were madly in love but what we were really doing was acting out a very special relationship with each other for the purpose of getting our perceived needs met, at the expense of really sharing love with ourselves and everyone else in the world. We were specially in love with each other to the exclusion of everyone else in the world. Sure, we loved other people, but our love for each other was special in our minds and, because of that, was a barrier to knowing our oneness with each other and everyone and everything.

Do you see from these two examples how special relationships work? They separate two people (or a family of people) from everyone else in the world and solidify those two people around common, shared aspects of getting the needs of the little made-up self met. From the two whole people, each person carves out, so to speak, and focuses on, those aspects of the other person's personality that facilitates getting her or his own perceived needs met. The rest of the two whole people, the unneeded personality traits, become insignificant and undesirable parts of the other person.

Each person is in "love" with those parts of the other person that meet their needs. Or, if it's not a love relationship but, say, a relationship between two friends, each person "likes" those parts of the other person that meet their needs. The discarded parts are, of course, still there in each person and ultimately become the focus for disagreements, arguments, non-compatibility, etc. resulting in strife and strain, and often dissolution, of the special relationship.

Expectations

There is no way that two made-up false selves can ever have a truly loving and holy relationship. What feels like love is the satisfaction of having your needs met. What feels like love is having every aspect of your perception of how your partner "should" be, being fulfilled by your partner and you fulfilling that role for your partner. That's a tall order, isn't it? And that's because it's based on expectations which are, of course, judgments. Judgments are fear-based and therefore relate to special relationships. Expectations are off-shoots of judgments, just a milder form of judgment.

To see if you are in a special relationship or not, just think of all of the ways that you see yourself as special and different from your partner. I know, you're a male and she's a female, or vice versa, or some other obvious difference, but I'm referring to the inner you. If you're like most humans on the planet, you'll see many different ways that you are different from your partner. Oh, and if you don't have a partner, then just use the most significant relationship in your life: your father, mother, brother, sister, grandparent, friend, etc. And that takes us to the idea of opposites. Let's consider that in the next chapter.

$1 + 1 = 1$

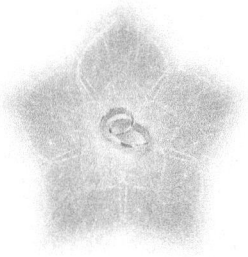

We meet ourselves time and again in a thousand disguises on the path of life.[18]
—CARL JUNG

I wrote a poem just recently about $1 + 1 = 1$. I didn't realize it was going to go in this book, but I see now that it belongs here. Here it is:

$1 + 1 = 1$
The reason $1 + 1 = 1$
And not $1 + 1 = 2$
Is because, when $1 + 1 = 2$
The 2 is always in conflict

> Never completely at peace
> And that is because 2 can never be joined
> As each 1 clings fearfully to its 1
> As they long and struggle for the love of 1
> Which never can be found as 2
>
> $1 + 1 = 1$
> Never takes, only gives
> $1 + 1 = 1$
> Never denies, and always receives
> $1 + 1 = 1$
> Only extends, only increases
> As all the hidden parts of each 1
> Gently unfold into the arms of loving oneness
> And what is left is a pure expression
> Of attributes of the Divine
> And what is gone, never was
> Never to be dreamed again

What this poem implies is that the hidden parts of each partner are able to be revealed because of the unconditional love and acceptance of each partner, just as I explained in Chapter Five. The reason hidden parts can gently unfold into the arms of loving oneness is that unconditional love and acceptance is free of judgment. And in the absence of judgment, there is only oneness. Just as it takes two to tango, it takes two to judge. Without judgment, there is only one.

Losing the Battle and the War

The conflict of two is that each partner is fearfully clinging to their own sense of self. It does feel like a life or death struggle, as I explained in Chapter Nine, because what's at stake *is* the self. And that is a losing battle because the only "gain" there is in keeping a sense of self, in a self that doesn't exist, is the illusion that the made-up self does exit. So to win that battle is, ironically, and paradoxically, to lose the battle and the war.

Once all hidden parts of two partners are revealed and accepted, they no longer have to be hidden in one partner nor acted out by the other partner. I will explain how that works in a moment. With everything about each other wholly revealed, each partner is able to freely express everything about themselves. And, even more importantly, since the previously hidden aspects are no longer hidden because those aspects are no longer a source of fear for each respective partner, they also dissolve from the consciousness of each partner that was holding the hidden aspect.

The hidden aspects of each partner's personality were merely false beliefs about themselves. Once the truth of the false belief is revealed, that it is false and not real, it is no longer valued as a secret to hang on to and is easily and naturally released from consciousness. Can you see how a holy relationship facilitates, and is a vehicle for, unconditional love and acceptance of yourself and, from there, for your partner?

Your Partner as Surrogate for the World

For example, once I revealed to Barbara my belief that there was something wrong with me, and she unconditionally and unequivocally demonstrated to me that she loved and accepted me even though I had that belief about myself, it was like a giant exhale of relief that I didn't have to hide myself from Barbara anymore. The most important person in the world to me loved and accepted me, all of me, unconditionally. And, since I had been hiding myself from the world, Barbara, as a surrogate for the world, helped me to be myself out in the world. Furthermore, I realized the false belief that there was something wrong with me was about the false self I made up that I previously thought was real. From there, it was an easy step to realize there *was* something wrong with me.

I believed in a false self that was not real and naturally I would think there was something wrong with me because there was something wrong with the me that I thought was me: it was false, not real. It didn't exist. And guess who helped me to see this about myself? Barbara did, of course, my partner in our holy relationship. Her vision was clear because it was not about her directly. Finally, the thing that was wrong with me was my belief in a self that didn't exist.

The whole idea loosened in my mind. I finally began

to laugh at it. I would say to myself and Barbara: "There *is* something wrong with me. I've believed in something that doesn't exist." And that little self began to crumble. I had taken the illusion of a made-up self into the light of truth and, in that light, the false belief dissolved. What emerged was a true belief in my mind that I am the Self that God created and in that Self there is never anything wrong or bad.

Do you see the power of that? Here's Barbara's example, different form, same underlying content.

Once Barbara revealed to me her belief that she was invisible, and she realized that was about a false self that was so false that it caused her to feel invisible, she realized there *was* something wrong with that false belief: it was false, not real. It didn't exist. And guess who finally suggested to Barbara that she didn't exist? It was me, but only after she first taught me what I've described just above about my false belief being rooted in a self that doesn't exist.

The thing that was actually invisible about her was her belief in a self that didn't exist. That whole idea loosened in her mind. She began to laugh at it. She would say to herself and to me: "I really *don't* exist. The "I" that I've been believing in really doesn't exist." And her little self began to crumble. The illusion of her made-up self was taken into the light of truth and, in that light, her false self dissolved. What emerged in her mind was the same thing that emerged in my mind, that she was the Self that God created and she knew that Self was real and did exist.

Illusion and its emotion of fear has unlimited numbers of mental, emotional and physical forms; after all, they are made up from our unlimited mind. But the underlying content is always the same: an illusion and a belief in a false self, or ego. My form was the belief that there was something wrong with me. Barbara's was that she was invisible. The underlying content of both forms was our belief in the illusion that we were the false self that we made up in our mind. And under all illusory content is the real content of truth: who and what we really are.

Hidden Parts: Revealed and Accepted

Now back to the idea that once all hidden parts of two partners are revealed and accepted, they no longer have to be hidden in one partner nor acted out by the other partner.

When two people come together in a relationship of any kind, there are always contrasting personality traits in each person. These contrasts are usually accentuated the most in committed couple relationships. I do know what it feels like to believe that you and your partner are exactly the same and that this sameness will blissfully carry you through the rest of your life. Barbara and I had that feeling for a long time. My ego did quietly surface in the LAX airport after our first trip to Hawaii, but I subdued it for a long time after. Eventually, both of our egos noisily surfaced in our relationship and the real work of our special relationship, and the transformation into a holy relationship, began.

It took us over 20 years (I know that's not very encouraging, but if you see it as a process, an adventure of love, instead of something to accomplish, it is encouraging) to feel like we were the same again. By then the sameness was an integration of everything we had learned together about ourselves and each other and it felt like a continual flow of love. When two people "join together for learning purposes . . . The relationship is holy because of that purpose . . . The demarcations they have drawn between their roles, their minds, their bodies, their needs, their interests, and all the differences they thought separated them from one another, fade and grow dim and disappear"[19]

Differences as Stepping Stones

The more mature and experienced with relationships you are, the easier it is for you to recognize the differences in you and your partner. So somewhere between the blindness of blissfully blended emotions that feel like love and the wise discernment of relationship maturity and self-awareness, each person in a couple relationship can eventually discover the differences between themselves and their partner. Learning to understand what these differences are about provide stepping stones to a happy, loving, holy relationship. Galvanizing around acceptance of your differences and rejection of your partner's provide stepping stones to a miserable, fearful, special relationship.

One very happy way to handle personality differences in a committed couple relationship is to unconditionally accept the differences in each other. With acceptance, there is no conflict. This is a great approach because if you can truly accept your partner's differences, they won't bother you and you'll be happier than if they did bother you. However, this approach doesn't get you to a holy relationship because you're still seeing your partner as separate from you. If s/he is different from you, you are obviously not the same, or one.

A better approach is to realize that you and your partner are, at your core, exactly the same as each other. You are both the changeless light of love that God extended into creation as His being, or spirit. In the dream of separation, you are two *aspects* of that changeless light of love, but you *are* that changeless light of love nonetheless. And you've both chosen the parents and family, or no family, you were going to be born into and all of those influences that implies. You've each taken on a temporary personality that best suits your intention of learning for this lifetime.

Acting Out Roles

So essentially, you're each acting out a role that you've come here to experience in this lifetime. And you've each attracted people and circumstances, from the time you were born until this very moment, that best facilitate the experiences you need in order to live the purpose for which you are here this lifetime. And the partner you have now, or have had in the past, or will have in the future, or the non-partner friend, family member or other significant relationship in your life has exactly the kind of personality, and vice versa, to best stimulate and facilitate your mutual growth according to the purpose for which you are here.

Once you realize that you and your partner are each playing a role in each other's life, the next step is to identify the significant traits that your partner has that you think you don't have and vice versa. What you will find are positive traits of your partner that you believe you don't have and also negative traits of your partner that you also believe you don't have and vice versa.

The Swiss psychiatrist, Carl Jung, referred to the positive traits as our "positive shadow" and the negative traits as our "negative shadow" or just "shadow" traits.[20] The truth is, we have the creative potential within us to develop and express all of the positive and negative traits of our partner. Since we are the extension of source, or God, into creation we have, by definition, all of the attributes of God. And by attributes I don't mean human characteristics like funny or serious, but aspects of the Divine that are abstract, like creativity, love, power, joy, peace, unlimitedness, freedom, etc.

So with the Divine aspect of creativity as part of our very being, we are able to take on characteristics of our partner that we have been hiding from ourselves. The potential was there all along. With the recognition of this ability, we can look at the positive traits of our partner that we have admired in her or him, but denied in ourselves, and realize we have that potential within ourselves also.

Positive Shadow Traits

One of my positive shadow traits that Barbara exhibited so beautifully was thinking for herself. I looked out into the world, to people that I admired and respected, as a mirror for how I *should* think and act. Once I learned about this positive shadow aspect of my personality, I learned from Barbara how she thought for herself, made decisions, took action and had the courage of her convictions to create the life she wanted to live.

As I opened fully to thinking for myself and began practicing it, we had a shift in our relationship that allowed Barbara to relax more as the strategist of our relationship as I took on more of that role in the process of learning how to think for myself and for us as a couple. My positive shadow aspect of Barbara thinking for herself came out of the shadow and into the light of my conscious mind. That difference between Barbara and I dissolved.

One of Barbara's positive shadow traits that I exhibited so well for her was my resourcefulness. Barbara did not see herself as resourceful and admired my resourcefulness. In identifying my resourcefulness as a potential within herself, she easily developed a belief in herself that she could be resourceful. As she practiced being resourceful, like with business or personal projects, she discovered that she was resourceful. In fact, she became amazingly resourceful. Because of that, it was no longer my responsibility to always be the resourceful one in our relationship and Barbara's positive shadow of resourcefulness was transformed from a potential in her unconscious mind to a reality in her conscious mind.

Negative Shadow Traits

The negative, or dark, shadow traits work the same way but have an additional step to them.

One of the shadow traits that I believed to be negative that I unconsciously hid from myself was anger. Barbara was the angry one in our relationship. She played that role in our relationship. If Barbara had a problem, no matter what it was, her first line of defense was to be angry. She might want to throw a computer out of a window (do you know that one?) or hit a keyboard with her fist or vent relentlessly about someone in her life that was "causing" her pain.

The more Barbara would escalate into anger the more I would cringe. It actually terrified me to feel Barbara's anger (do you know that one?), even if it wasn't about me and you can imagine how terrified I felt if her anger was about me.

Cause and Effect versus Effect and Blame

Of course, Barbara eventually identified her anger as a projection of an inner hurt that she wasn't taking responsibility for and in the last healthy months of her life never got angry at all. And that is the additional step that is involved with negative shadow traits. Once brought to the light, and consciously identified as problematic, they have to be transformed into a love-based belief from a fear-based belief by the partner that first exhibited that trait.

In this example, Barbara was afraid to take responsibility for her anger. By lovingly deciding to take responsibility for her anger, she realized she was really angry at herself because she was judging herself for whatever experience she was having in her life that was causing the anger. By dropping the judgment, and unconditionally loving and accepting herself in each situation, her anger dissolved.

This process also allowed her to take responsibility for what she was creating in her life instead of blaming other people, or situations, and being angry at them for the experiences she was having. A person becomes very masterful when they finally accept responsibility for everyone and everything in their life, without judgment. Our intelligence is then focused on cause and effect, instead of effect and blame. It also facilitates your conversion from victim to the master of your fate.

Accepting Your Negative Shadow Trait

Barbara's healing about anger also took a dramatic turn for the better when I learned the value of recognizing and owning my anger, instead of repressing (unconsciously) or suppressing (consciously) it.

Once I started allowing and feeling and communicating anger in my life, Barbara's need to do so diminished drastically. We both noticed it right away and knew that she, at deep unconscious purpose-driven levels of her mind, no longer needed to play the role of the angry one in our relationship. We eventually became very adroit with anger and could feel it, identify its cause within ourselves and change the belief that was causing us to project anger out onto someone or something else.

One of the shadow traits that Barbara believed to be negative that she unconsciously hid from herself was the belief that she couldn't make a mistake. That was part of her always being about excellence. I was the one that made mistakes in our relationship. I played that role in our relationship.

However, having been a perfectionist for years, and the pain of that, finally got me to see that the only thing perfect in this life was our underlying Divinity and that nothing in the dream of life, the illusion of form, really mattered and was certainly not perfect.

I know that sounds harsh and I do have compassion for everyone and everything on the planet. But, ultimately, I realized that it is our underlying Divinity that we are here to learn about and everything else is just changing forms, like bodies and relationships and nature and everything else that is part of life, all contributing toward our learning who and what we really are. This awareness helped me to see "failure" as simply an experience and thus transform the fear of failure into the love of experience. I no longer ran from mistakes. Rather, I embraced life.

So as Barbara saw me being able to make mistakes, large or small, and not judge myself for them, and even laugh at them, she began to allow herself to acknowledge mistakes that she previously would just accept with a sigh and a "whatever". She was able to see mistakes as just experiences and to love and accept herself right through them. What was previously hidden in her shadow as a fear of being "wrong" or "bad" by making a mistake became a conscious acceptance of the imperfection of life and herself as a joyful liver of life. I came to believe that the only perfection in the dream of life is the perfect way all the imperfection works together.

As Barbara began to acknowledge mistakes, instead of deny them or project them onto me or someone or something else, I no longer seemed to make them. Of course I still made them, but they were no longer an issue. And, as with Barbara's anger, we both knew that I, at deep unconscious purpose-driven levels in my mind, no longer needed to play the role of the one that always made mistakes in our relationship.

A Turning Point

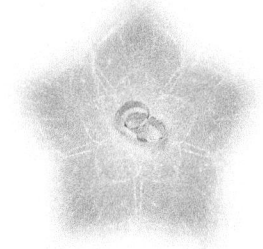

A healed mind is relieved of the belief that it must plan, although it cannot know the outcome which is best, the means by which it is achieved, nor how to recognize the problem that the plan is made to solve. It must misuse the body in its plans until it recognizes this is so. But when it has accepted this as true, then is it healed, and let's the body go.[21]

—A COURSE IN MIRACLES

For our twentieth wedding anniversary, Barbara and I went to New England for the first time. September first was our anniversary and we allowed plenty of time after that to be able to wander up to northern Maine, then over through New Hampshire and then back down through Vermont, Massachusetts and Connecticut to JFK for our flight back home.

Reiki Massage

In the White Mountains of northern New Hampshire we stayed at an elegant inn that had a spa downstairs on the bottom floor. I have long since had a deep appreciation for massages, particularly alternative types, like Reiki and chakra balancing. The brochure said there was a Reiki practitioner there so I called and made an appointment.

Barbara had given up on massages years before because she had been injured in a massage once and was not one to repeat a painful experience. That was one of the beautiful, and wise, things about her: when she experienced pain, she always went to work immediately figuring out what it was in her consciousness that created and/or attracted that pain and then made the appropriate change in her consciousness so that she didn't need that pain anymore. I, on the other hand, have tended to accept pain as a way of life and have needed increased, focused pain to get my attention so that I would change it. I had become her masseuse. I knew nothing about massage, except from having them, and I don't consider myself as a hands-on bodywork kind of person. But with Barbara I could always find the knots and sore spots in her body and could always gently and easily work them out of her body. So, as usual, Barbara scheduled a facial.

What I experienced with my Reiki massage was a master healer in the woman that worked on my body. I never talk in massages. I meditate, become one with the process, let go and allow myself to go inwardly as deep as possible. And now that I think about it, I can see how that probably helps the masseuse to connect with me in the most holistic way possible. It was an extraordinary massage, in the category of a few life-changing massages I'd had in the past.

When the bodywork was finished, the masseuse gave me feedback about what she experienced during the massage. She didn't explain the process to me, but I knew from other similar experiences that she had connected intuitively with my energy field and was able to communicate with the deepest levels of my being. It was basically a description and affirmation of my talents as a communicator.

She also told me my intuitive abilities were very open and she encouraged me to trust my intuition and to act on it as much as possible. I told her I had been practicing that for some time now and that I appreciated her recognition of my openness to trusting my intuition.

She also said she saw that I was a shaman in a previous lifetime and that I had innate shamanistic abilities that could be brought out in this lifetime. She encouraged me emphatically to pursue this path and even gave me her personal copy of a book about shamanism. I told her that I already knew my shaman animal guide was an eagle named Blye. I didn't tell her I knew that because of Barbara's ability to transcend the physical and communicate with entities on the other side or what I call the astral. Barbara kept that very private and I was honoring that as I always did. I did ask the masseuse if she had time to do a Reiki massage with Barbara and she said she did.

On two previous occasions in Sedona, Barbara had agreed to alternative types of massages because of my experiences with the masseuses and they were life-changing for both of us. Because of those two previous experiences, and my enthusiasm and conviction that this Reiki massage would be a great experience for Barbara, she wanted to have the Reiki massage. She and I both knew that she would be able to "see" whatever the masseuse would be seeing, or reading, about Barbara's energy and that added an extra measure of mystery for us both.

When Barbara got back to the room from the massage, she was glowing from the experience. I knew she would have been deep into a trance state during the massage and the peace and rejuvenation from that alone would have been worth the time invested in the experience. She did look rejuvenated and her whole body seemed to glow. What she reported was something mysterious and something surprising.

A Dozen Light Masters

After the bodywork, she and the masseuse discussed what they had seen and they saw exactly the same thing. About a dozen astral beings, basically beings of light with enough definition to their astral bodies that each could be distinguished individually, had encircled Barbara's body and seemed to, individually and collectively, insert what appeared to be rod-like spheres of light, or light energy, into the lower part of Barbara's abdomen. After quite a while, they stopped and left as gently as they had originally appeared.

Barbara and the masseuse could only surmise that some kind of healing process had taken place. The masseuse was visibly and emotionally shaken by the experience. She reported that she could feel the energy of the astral beings and that they seemed to exude wisdom and love. She was in awe of Barbara because of that experience and told her that she had never experienced such powerful extrasensory abilities in a person before.

Barbara was never in awe of her powers and, probably because this was so commonplace for Barbara, it did not hold the same emotional charge for Barbara as it did for the masseuse. Nevertheless, Barbara was intrigued by the astral beings because all of her previous experiences with the astral were in direct communication with that type of light being and she had learned a lot from those experiences.

When we got home I spent a week or two reflecting on the shamanism thing trying to decide if I wanted to pursue that path or not. In the end, I got clarity that the path I was on was the one for me and that any shamanistic abilities I may have were already integrated into me and that it didn't serve me or my purpose for being here to develop them as a singular focus.

Anything and Everything is Possible

Barbara and I both still wondered about the astral beings. Then sometime in late October or early November Barbara told me she was spotting, having light vaginal bleeding. That soon developed into a regular period, yet Barbara had been post-menopausal for a long time. Now keep in mind that Barbara and I both believed, despite the laws of science, that anything and everything was possible at all times about anything and everything.

We knew that the laws of science were how mankind, the collective unconscious of the human race, limited itself so as to "prove" its separateness from source or God. We had worked for years to manifest unlimited abundance in the seemingly limited world that we lived in. So nothing ever surprised us in this regard and we always delighted at stories of people going beyond their seeming limits. From this joint frame of reference that we both had about how the world really worked, we were now wondering why she was having periods. And we also wondered if those astral beings in New Hampshire, that inserted the rods of light into her abdomen, had anything to do with the bleeding.

Isaac and Abraham

Our last dog, Isaac, only gone for about a year and still fresh in our minds, was scheduled to be "put down" by the Austin dog pound on the Saturday that we got him in 1996. Barbara convinced the manager of the facility to postpone that event until we got there and we always knew we saved Isaac's life by adopting him.

With Barbara's background of knowing the Bible very well, she knew the story in the Old Testament of God telling Abraham to kill his son, Isaac, as an offering to Him, and then withdrew the command after Abraham demonstrated his willingness to kill Isaac. Barbara told me the story, with "Sandy", the dog pound's name for Isaac, in the back seat of our car as we drove home to Houston from the pound. Once I heard the story of God, Abraham and Isaac, I agreed with Barbara to name him Isaac.

And now that we were wondering why Barbara, a menopausal woman of 56 years old, was having a period, we began to think of Sarah, Abraham's wife who was 90 years old when she gave birth to her son, Isaac. If Sarah could have a baby at 90 years old over 2,000 years ago when 90 years old was very, very old, why couldn't Barbara have a baby at 56 years old in the year 2009? We frolicked with this idea for about a month, perhaps a little less, and were ecstatic to consider the possibility of having a baby at our stage in life.

The idea of us having a baby faded away as we began to realize that Barbara was not having a period but was continuing to bleed, day after day after day. In fact, the bleeding got worse, about as maximal as you can imagine. So we found an OB/GYN whose write up online appealed to us and we made an appointment. It was now right before Christmas, 2009.

The Beginning Of The End

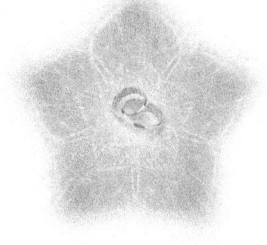

If you would but let the Holy Spirit tell you of the Love of God for you . . . you would experience the attraction of the eternal. No one can hear Him speak of this and long remain willing to linger here.[22]

—A Course in Miracles

When we returned from a Christmas trip in 2009, to visit family in Louisiana, there was an urgent sounding message from the doctor on our answering machine saying that we needed to make an immediate appointment to come in and see her, which we did. I will never forget how the words seemed to echo in my ears in slow motion when the doctor said, "You have cervical cancer. I can't help you with that. Here is the phone number of two university hospitals that can help you. I find each is equally good. Speak to both of them and see which one you like the best." It was the "cervical cancer" part that reverberated in my mind, of course.

Be Really Strong

Outside in the car, the first one to speak was Barbara. She said, "We're going to have to be really strong through this, Jimmie". I was struck by the calmness in her voice and knew that what she said was true. Little did I know at the time just how strong we both were going to have to be.

It turned out that Barbara didn't have cervical cancer and I apologize for the glimmer of hope that statement may stimulate in you. What Barbara had was uterine cancer, two different versions thereof. In our consultation with the female OB/GYN-oncologist that we had selected to work with, Barbara was told that she needed immediate surgery and, after that, a chemotherapy/radiation treatment plan would be recommended to her.

The surgery was reported as successful except for some minor tissue that was left behind that the doctor didn't think would be a future problem. Whether it was really a problem I'll never know. The surgery was major, the hospital stay was major and the recovery was major.

When Barbara was stable enough to return to the medical center for a treatment consultation, we were told that the type of chemotherapy she needed was so severe that it would take her body down to basically having very little immune system left and she would therefore need to be hospitalized during the entire course of treatment. Barbara declined the treatment on the spot. She knew she was not willing to go back into the hospital and asked for other options.

We came back a week later after the doctor had time to consult with her colleagues, who were OB/GYN-oncologists, oncologists and radiation oncologists. The new treatment protocol that was recommended was a course of five chemotherapy treatments, done on an out-patient basis in the medical center's chemotherapy treatment center. And radiation therapy was recommended after that. Barbara agreed to the chemotherapy and would decide about the radiation after that. After three chemotherapy treatments, Barbara had had enough and told the doctor she was not going to return. A CT scan and a MRI were done, as well as a biopsy, and all three showed Barbara's body to be cancer free. We were delighted. She declined the radiation therapy. And we were convinced the cancer would never come back.

As Barbara's physical condition got progressively better we reevaluated our lives. Barbara consciously made the decision to put meditation first in her life. I had long since valued as much meditation/introspection/reflection as possible by practicing being still and going deeply into the presence of now, of experiencing the holy instant. Barbara didn't need to "practice"; she had her own natural way of almost immediately being deeply into the presence of being and, in doing so, being able to communicate with entities on the other side.

Extrasensory Abilities

When Barbara was still conscious and alert, but in the "dying" process, I asked her if I could tell people about her extrasensory abilities. She said, "You can tell them anything you want", as I have now done, although I am holding back the entire experience of our relationship with our guides and what were referred to as other "interested parties" for a later book. I will use these examples in this book only as I believe they serve the purpose of illuminating a way to knowing how to create a holy relationship.

Barbara also wanted us to begin traveling on a regular basis as a way of using travel as a spiritual awakening. There was one particular place Barbara really wanted to experience and that was the resort in Northern India called "Ananda", which is located near the foothills of the Himalayan mountains and not far from the city of

Rishekesh, famous for its location on the holy Ganges river and where the Beatles spent time during their spiritual sojourn to India in the 60's.

Babaji

I had always heard that "ananda" means happiness or bliss in Sanskrit, and that made my attraction, or desire, to going to the Ananda resort even stronger. Barbara wanted to go there because she felt like we might be able to physically meet the sage, Babaji, not the contemporary, relatively young Babaji, but the centuries old Babaji that is featured in Paramahansa Yogananda's book, *Autobiography of a Yogi*. Barbara had been told years before by our guide that Babaji would visit us for the purpose of teaching us how to transcend bodily limitations.

Babaji did finally visit us, on three different occasions, two times through what I will call astral communication with Barbara, and one time through Barbara as his channel.

The first time, in the early 2000's, he came to Barbara via astral communication on a Sunday night when we were laying in bed together talking. She said, "Jimmie, Babaji is here." I sat up in bed, ecstatic to hear that Babaji had finally come. He said a few simple things about oneness to Barbara, for us, and concluded by telling Barbara that we were not yet ready for his training about the body but that he would return again.

Babaji came again, in 2009, via astral communication, after we had moved to California and gave us two beautifully meaningful, and powerful, teachings about our mind in relationship to our bodies. These were called, "Lesson One" and "Lesson Two" and more were to follow but we never reached that point. I will save the insights from those two readings for a future book, but will share here an inspiration from Babaji about oneness.

An Astral Intervention

On September 19, 2006, when we still lived in Houston, Babaji came to us and used Barbara as a channel for his voice. Here is what he said through Barbara to me and for us:

> *"Do you not understand the energy of two is one? There is an I in what you've been doing." I asked, "How do I let go of I?" He replied with, "Dive into the we. There's no other way. Dive into the all. There is no other way. The we is the way to the all and the all is the way to the we. Let go of I and dive into the all."*
>
> *Babaji then asked, "What do you have your eyes on?" "Me", I replied. "What does*

*Barbara have her eyes on?" "Us" was my
answer. "There you have it", he replied.*

*"My dear one, you think you are a separate
one and you're so mistaken and so afraid
to let go of that. I would just let go of that.
If you did, you would dive into the bliss of
oneness. There is no joy of being yourself in
separateness. You're honoring your ego instead
of honoring what you know and you will
never advance in that manner."*

*At this point I called Babaji "Holy Spirit"
because that is who I thought he was. I had
had discussions with the Holy Spirit and the
power and clarity of Babaji's voice caused
me to think he was the Holy Spirit. He
replied with, "My name is Babaji. I told you
I would come. I can't get past the emotions
to teach you about the physical. You've got
to let go of the concept of 'you' and become
a 'we'. That's a start. Then become an
'all' and there you have it. As you improve
emotionally, I can teach you physically. You
are weak emotionally. So fight your fights,*

> *overcome your emotions and surrender to the 'we'. Surrender to what is. You are already connected."*

Babaji confirmed for me what Barbara had always told me and wanted from me, to have my eyes focused on her and us, instead of myself. It was a wake-up call for me, an astral intervention, if you will, and it helped tremendously. And Barbara and I took the "we" part, and the "all" part, very seriously and it facilitated us deepening our desire for knowing the oneness that she and I knew we were.

Our aspiration was always to know ourselves as one and then to take that oneness out into the world and extend our sense of oneness to everyone and everything. We never did get to the "out into the world" part. Now we were living in California, in seclusion away from the world, and all we wanted, with the intervention of Barbara's near death through the cancer experience, was to know our oneness with our source, with God, and to take that awareness from within ourselves and extend it to each other as oneness.

Experiences versus Things

In this spirit did we write our second renewal of marriage vows, and commit to them, on New Year's Eve, 2009. And now that we believed that Barbara was free of cancer and we were reevaluating our lives, we wanted to bring ourselves out into the world with our idea of traveling as a spiritual awakening. We didn't know who we would meet, or where, or why, but we believed every step of our lives from then on would be some way of deepening our spiritual experience of life and our desire to know our oneness with each other, with our source, and with everyone and everything. To that end, we consciously committed to making experiences more important than things.

We decided to use our money to facilitate us moving through the world through travel as a spiritual awakening. We also decided to spend our money, and not hoard it, and to help other people with our money. We put our house up for sale (it didn't sell) so that we could get a smaller one so that we could use the extra money for travel and so that we didn't need to devote time and attention to our current much larger house and land.

A Bird Out of a Cage

Barbara felt like a bird out of a cage now, although she was still healing inside of her body from the massive surgery. We were never to have sex again because of that. Our last sexual experience was on a shopping trip to Las Vegas in October right before the bleeding started. The physical intimacy was no accident, occurring right before the physical bleeding. It was like the beginning of the end for us, in the physical; we just didn't know it yet.

During this post-surgery and post-chemotherapy healing period, Barbara and I were both focused on letting go of everything that blocked us from knowing our oneness with God and each other. I knew she had been wondering about sex and so had I. One day, during this healing period, she rubbed her body gently against mine and I simply said, "Yes, I've been wondering about sex myself." Her rubbing was an indication to me that she had finished her contemplation about sex and saw it like food and other earthly pleasures, not to mention the expression of love through the body when love is present, where there is giving and receiving and no taking involved.

I was using my contemplations about sex as a mental lubricant to help me release my guilt for believing I had separated from God and the oneness of His creation. I saw that as long as I was on the Earth, living in physical form through a body, that I used food and water, even air, as part of the physical forms that I used to keep the body alive and healthy. And, since there is actually no innate difference between physical form of any kind, with it all being crystallized energy into various forms, then the enjoyment of sex is no different than the enjoyment of food.

One Connected Energy

Now that I live in Northern California by myself, I have met several people that have had the experience of seeing everything around them, people and things, as one connected energy through the use of either LSD or mushrooms. I've never used either, and probably never will, and am not advocating their use here, although I also have no judgment about their use or non-use. Each person has reported to me basically the same thing, that they were able to see everyone and everything as one energy, all vibrating and shimmering and colorful, and all connected. One person described it as "seeing everything made out of the same atoms". And each was awakened by their experience into a definite awareness that there is a spirituality, a light, an energy, beyond the confines of the body that connects everyone and everything.

Barbara once had this type of experience without any outside stimulus to get the mind out of the way so that her inner being could have such an experience. We were in Sedona hiking on one of our favorite mountains when we reached the base of a peak that we had read about in local Sedona literature. The peak was known to have a large crystal embedded within it and thus facilitative of awakening inner energies if someone is open and receptive enough.

I could feel the energy as a mild, soothing, uplifting energy that facilitated a lovely meditation as I sat there on the side of the mountain. Barbara's experience was quite different. She went into a trance and was guided by our astral guide to a vibratory level where she could see, with her eyes open, the mountain and the entire surroundings, as pure vibrating energy. She knew she was not seeing with the body's eyes but with an inner vision. And she knew she was seeing the essence of the physical forms surrounding her, the underlying light from which everything in the physical universe is made.

Inner Vision

Barbara began having this same type of inner vision during her post-surgery, post-chemo period in 2010. She would meditate for several hours a day and often I would see her in a meditative trance with her eyes open. During these meditations, and also when she was not meditating, Barbara began having short, spontaneous experiences just like the one I've described when we were in Sedona. She knew that something was happening to her consciousness, that she was expanding, opening up more, awakening. I told her I thought she was reaching new levels of higher consciousness and that I was very happy for her. Looking back on these experiences, I believe they were all part of Barbara's end-of-physical-life as she was being prepared to leave the physical.

In April of 2010 Barbara and I had some insights in meditation that are reflective of where our minds were at that time. On April 25 Barbara received this: "I gave you life. I would never take it away. There is no death. The body has no life except for Me enlivening it. There is no life apart from Me." On April 27, I asked, "What is life?", and the response from spirit was, "It is the extension of Myself into manifestation as you." We knew that didn't mean our bodies or the life "time" that we were currently in. We knew that related to our beliefs about "life" and "death" and that our minds were being expanded.

On June 6, 2010 Barbara and I were meditating on the deck outside our bedroom in chairs next to each other. Barbara opened her eyes and said to me, "I think I have found my Self." I didn't say anything because she had already closed her eyes again and was back in deep meditation. Two days later we were meditating side-by-side again. I opened my eyes as she began to speak. She said, "I have found my Self". I asked, "What does it feel like?" Her response was, ". . . powerful . . . loved . . . innocence . . . joy." Barbara's meditations had amazed me for over two decades. With these two meditations, I knew that Barbara was waking up from the dream of separation. I knew she was experiencing, in meditation, the oneness of all that is. I wondered how much more time she had here in the physical.

Living from Spirit, as Spirit

This relates to a holy relationship because Barbara's expanding consciousness seemed to be melting away the rough edges of her personality. She seemed to me to be living more and more from spirit and less and less through her personality. As her personality dissolved, spirit emerged.

This related to me in two ways. Barbara was losing all judgment of me and she seemed to be merging with me, integrating me into her. For example, the old Barbara was always fixated on time, figuring everything out so she could get everything done and could then relax. The new Barbara was relaxed all the time and only concerned herself with the barest of essentials, like food, but with no attachment to time.

With the old Barbara, I used to want to ramble around the country roads of this rural county we lived in just for the experience of exploring, but I would only have the courage to perhaps mention half a sentence about that desire which would fall on deaf ears that were loyal to Barbara's time management.

With the new Barbara, I sensed her inner freedom and began saying things like, "I'd love to explore this side road to see where it goes before we go home" and she'd say, "Go ahead. That'll be fun." And we'd ramble around, and wander around, until we'd eventually find our way back home sharing a sense of freedom and unlimited abundance because, after all, we were living in the "time and financial freedom" that we had always wanted.

Merging Personalities

What was happening to Barbara and I in mid-2010, post-surgery and post-chemo, is that our personalities were merging. And here are the two best examples I can think of.

Previously, if I would stimulate anything within Barbara that would relate to her believing she didn't exist, like not hearing her, i.e., listening but not "hearing", or even just not listening so that she'd have to repeat herself, she would bristle and at least come back with some version of a mild "attack" in order to try to get me to be the way she wanted me to be. With all of the work she had done to replace her primal fear of not existing with certainty of who and what she really was, all of that previous pain had now vanished and surfaced as only a mild shadow of an old worn out habit. So now, with my stimulus of non-attention toward Barbara (I promise you my non-attention was now very slight and soon to go away completely; it was there only until she didn't need it anymore.), she would only slightly take notice and as I would begin to apologize she would say something like, "No. You didn't do anything. That's about me." And would smile and give me a gentle touch. The first time she did that, in about May or June of 2010, I knew right then and there that she was finally healed of all the old pain. And I was so very happy for her.

Natural and Easy Affections

The best example I have about me merging with Barbara is this one, also in May or June of 2010. For all of our 22 years together I had many different fond little names for her. They were little affections based on some personality trait of hers that I knew and loved. But I also knew that I had a little bit of a hold back, way down deep inside, that prevented me from unleashing the deepest, and fondest, affections for her in any given moment. Only when I was occasionally completely unleashed, released from my own inner demons, which felt like inner tensions and stress and therefore an inward pull toward defending myself, did I really feel the fullness of affection for Barbara. I know that sounds sad and it was sad. It was my addiction to pain as a way of unconsciously keeping my ego, my false self, alive and, in so doing, projecting the cause of my pain onto Barbara.

Finally I knew that had all changed, had all finally been dissolved, when I walked from the kitchen to the dining room, put a plate of food down in front of Barbara and said, "Here Angel". In that moment, I could feel the unbridled love and affection for Barbara that was flowing from me to her. I had never called her "Angel" before. I knew I was finally loving Barbara fully at all times and not just intermittently. I could feel the love palpably. And I could feel Barbara receiving the love as she looked up at me and very slowly said to me as she gazed in my eyes, "I like when you call me Angel". That broke my heart wide open and I returned with, "I like to call you that too. You *are* an angel." From that moment forward, I had nothing but natural and easy affections for Barbara in a way I never had before.

Unlimited Possibilities

Do I believe you have to have a partner with extrasensory abilities like Barbara in order to have a holy relationship? No I don't, not at all. But when two people care more about their relationship with God than anything, and their relationship with each other as an extension of that prime relationship with God, there is no telling what kinds of unlimited possibilities will open up in each of them.

Once the value has gone from ego to God, or the Christ within that we really are, from illusion to truth, from fear to love, all consciously and joined with this united purpose, each partner in the holy relationship is now unfolding in miraculous ways because the milieu of the relationship is no longer fear, but love. It is no longer illusion, but truth. It is no longer ego, but God. And love, truth and God are all the same: unlimited in every way.

And what that can look like in the physical world in a holy relationship is something that will be uniquely expressed, using the beginning framework of the relationship and the people involved, by spirit that is flowing through and as the holy relationship. And you are just as holy as me or Barbara or your partner or your future partner. Just as your partner, or future partner, is just as holy as you. The relationship will be miraculous because you have chosen it to be so.

I offered for Barbara and me to go to India, to Ananda, now that the surgery and chemotherapy was over. But she said she wasn't ready because she could tell she was still healing deep inside of her body and didn't want to take such a long and potentially arduous trip right then. She did want to go to Hawaii, though, which, with Sedona, were our two favorite places in the world, as a celebration trip for her now being well.

In Hawaii we rented a two-person covered double beach chair thing right on the beach every day for a full week. And we stayed out there reading *A Course in Miracles* and related spiritual material, meditating, talking, napping and just generally communing with spirit, each other and nature all week long. We played tennis, went swimming, took walks, went shopping, drove out into nature and had great open-air dinners every night. But during a several hour period every day we huddled together in our little mini-house on the beach, letting nature influence us as we absorbed the beauty and peace of Hawaii down to our very bones.

We came back rejuvenated and began preparing for my mother and step-father, and sister and brother-in-law, to come for a several day visit in July. When we were all together, we played like kids and had a ball and enjoyed each other's company. Then on the last night of that family visit, Barbara began feeling a little weak and sickly. The next morning she did feel sick, told everyone goodbye as they left, then went to bed with what she believed was the stomach flu.

The Gewürztraminer Popsicle

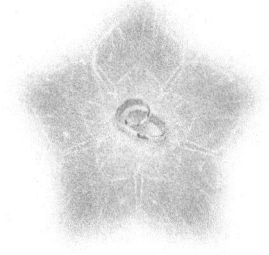

Because love is the most powerful force in the universe it is also the most frightening until it has been entered into completely. That generally happens just about at the finishing point of the final life.[23]

—IMMANUEL

For the next ten days we thought Barbara had the flu. Since it was in her stomach, she called it the "stom-

The Gewürztraminer Popsicle ⌁ 179

ach flu". Because she had been in pharmaceuticals for so many years, and was like a virtual doctor in my mind, I believed it was the flu at first. Knowing Barbara, she probably knew it related to the previous cancer and was just trying to stay out of the hospital. She hated being in the hospital. But anyway, I was probably in denial at first but as Barbara got worse we began to talk about going to see a doctor.

She told me she was in regular communication with "spirit" and that He would tell her if she needed to go to a doctor. This caused me to think that Barbara's body would be healed from all of the inner work she was doing during this time. But she did get worse and finally she told me, "Spirit says it's time to see a doctor". We went to the local internal medicine guy that I had been to before. We told him her recent medical history and he quickly did many tests and concluded that she needed to go into the hospital for more tests. That's when I convinced Barbara that it was time for me to call her OB/GYN-oncologist from the hospital where she had previously been treated. She returned my call immediately. It was after 5 P.M. on a Thursday night. She told me she didn't have office hours on Friday but that she would see Barbara anyway and asked when we could be there. Barbara said 2:00 P.M. in the background and the doctor agreed.

As soon as the doctor saw Barbara she looked concerned. After the pelvic exam she said she believed that the tumor had returned and that we had two choices. She could schedule an outpatient CT Scan which would take until the next week to put her on the schedule. Or Barbara could be admitted that night to the hospital and a CT Scan would be done in the morning. Barbara agreed to be admitted to the hospital. Now we were really wondering about the experience Barbara had during the Reiki massage in New Hampshire, the beings of light and those mysterious rods of light that were put into her body.

Late the next morning the doctor knocked on the door and walked solemnly into Barbara's hospital room. We knew that she now had the results of the CT Scan. The doctor sat on the side of the bed, took Barbara's hand, looked her lovingly in the eyes and said, "The tumor has returned. It is two and a half times larger than the first one. There is nothing we can do. If we did surgery, it is so big and so entangled with the other organs that it is highly likely that you would not make it through the surgery. It is inoperable. We are going to refer you to hospice in the county where you live. They will take care of you and will keep you comfortable. And I will be in communication with hospice to make sure you have everything you need." I asked a few administrative questions about hospice and when we were finished the Dr. hugged us both goodbye and silently left the room while closing the door behind her.

Barbara's New Life

Barbara turned over to the left side of the bed, where I was sitting, looked me in the eyes and said, "I'm excited about my new life." Have you ever known, or heard about, anyone saying they were looking forward to their new life outside of this physical world when they were on their virtual deathbed? I have, and that is part of why I am sharing this story with you.

Barbara's Last Admonition to Me

She paused a few moments then said, "You are going to have to love yourself enough to know what you want and have yourself, and everyone around you, honor that." True to form for Barbara, she knew exactly what to say to me, in precise, summary form, exactly what I needed to hear. I now refer to that advice to me as Barbara's "last admonition" to me. I knew then that her counsel to me was exactly what I needed. It resonated deeply. And as I've lived my life without her being physically here, the thing that helps me more than anything is that last admonition of Barbara's for me.

As I write this, Barbara's last admonition is still my screen saver on my computer and, in fact, it has just popped up as I have sat here reflecting on what to write here. And since I don't believe in accidents, or accidental coincidences, I take that screen saver pop up as a nudge to me that it does serve you, also, in some way, to know this admonition from Barbara. Perhaps you might receive it as an admonition to you?

Barbara's Last Admonition to You

Barbara's admonition to me is, perhaps, equally important to you. And here is why.

On June 23, 2006 Barbara and I had finished dinner and were sitting at our dining table talking. Suddenly her body began to move, as it had many times before, in such a way that I knew she was being prepared to allow our guide, Petrov, to use her body to communicate with me.

After she was stilled, her body began to be animated again and, with her eyes open, and from a voice I had never heard before, came the words, "Who are you and what do you want?" I had years of experience of talking to entities from the other side through Barbara, especially Petrov, and I knew this was someone new. However, I was unnerved by the power of the voice and by the words the voice was saying and I thought it might be an unfriendly entity that was asking me who I was and what did I want with him so I responded with, "Who are you?" The voice responded with, "Who are you and what do you want?" I said again, "Who are you?"

This time the voice said, "Who are you and what do you want? Those are the only two questions that matter. These are the questions I ask you in the stillness, over and over. It is the Holy Spirit. Can't you tell? Here, hold my hands and feel me." I took Barbara's outreached hands and held them in mine. He said, "Can you feel me? Don't you recognize me?" With eyes closed, I felt deeply into the moment and could feel my energy as one with the powerful energy coming through Barbara's hands. I responded with, "Yes, I can feel you."

The voice then said, "So who are you and what do you want?" I responded with, "I am the Son of God and I want to live in truth."

He responded with, "You are all that ever was. You are all that is. You are all that ever will be. So why do you defend against something that's not real? You think it up in your head and it becomes true in your reality. It is appearances that you're afraid of".

The "reading" continued with an interchange between He and I relating to my self-doubt and belief in appearances. He revealed some very beautiful and powerful things to me that I would only want to write about if I were giving more background and in-depth explanation about readings from the other side and my experience from them. But since that is not the purpose of this book, I'm just going to say that who you are and what you want, in this book, relate directly to wanting and having a holy relationship. Knowing who you are, and therefore, by definition, who the other person truly is, *is* what a holy relationship is. The "what do you want" is an easy extension from that.

Our Remaining Time Together

On the drive back home from the Sacramento hospital Barbara told me that she wanted to spend our remaining time together with just us. Behind that statement was a lot of what I already knew about Barbara. Barbara's relationship with God was first and our relationship was second and a vehicle for, and a part of, our relationship with God. I also knew that Barbara never, ever, wasted her time. That was one of the very first things that I learned about her years ago. She had an exquisitely fine tuned sense of time and its importance to her. And as I said in earlier chapters, Barbara always did everything fast.

So I knew her leaving the body was not going to take very long. I knew it was not going to be a long, drawn out process. That just wasn't Barbara. Knowing all of this about Barbara, I instantly knew why she wanted our remaining time together to be by ourselves. In Barbara's mind, everything else was finished. The time remaining was for us and she wanted no distractions. And that is how it was.

Barbara's remaining time in her body was to be a short five weeks. And I believe Barbara gave those short, but intense, five weeks to me as a vehicle for me to wholly focus on her as a way of preparing me for my new life after she left the physical. I also believe those entities in New Hampshire had something to do with facilitating Barbara having a way to leave the physical when she was ready.

Hospice

The hospice nurse came the day after we got home, explained everything to me, and visited briefly with Barbara. From then on the nurse, a very loving and helpful person, came to me, and Barbara if necessary, twice a week to deliver medicine and to see if I needed help with anything in caring for Barbara. The manager of hospice, also a nurse, also came by once a couple of weeks later, and she explained to me what to expect during the final stages of Barbara leaving her body. I was basically trained how to be a quasi, or virtual, hospice nurse because of Barbara's insistence on having no one around her except me, unless it was absolutely necessary. So we kept all visits by hospice short and they mostly interacted with me.

I was trained in how and when to administer many different medicines to Barbara. But it was only as the . . . I just can't use the word "death", or "dying", without putting it in quotes because Barbara and I didn't believe in "death" . . . "dying" process deepened that I became acutely aware of the responsibility I had, and its consequences, in administering morphine to Barbara.

Barbara's Life in My Hands

Both of the nurses had told me that she would begin to need more and more morphine and they explained how and when to use it. They also explained that there were no limits on how often to administer the morphine when the end was near. They made predictions of how that would work and, in the end, that was exactly how it did work. So, in the end, I was acutely aware that the morphine was not only alleviating any pain but was also helping the body to shut down. And that was the part that was so very sensitive to me. It was like Barbara's life was in my hands and, at the same time, all I wanted to do was to keep her out of pain.

While Barbara was still sleeping in our bed with me, at the beginning of this final five week period of our lives together, we talked about moving to Oregon so that she could take advantage of the state's end-of-life law that allowed terminal patients to be given a lethal combination of medicines in order to end their life when they wanted. Barbara asked me to research it and the research showed that she'd have to be living in Oregon for a six month period before she would be eligible for that program. We knew she didn't have that much time. So we never did really make a decision as to whether or not she would use the end-of-life program because of the six month residency rule.

Looking back on it, I know that we would not have gone to Oregon because what Barbara was doing during her "dying" process was creating the precise circumstance that would fully facilitate me giving to her completely and totally and, in so doing, finally letting go of the self-focus that I had so long held onto in our relationship.

I also told Barbara that I didn't want to be here by myself after she left so we talked about the possibility of me ending my life right after hers would be over. She never really gave me an opinion about that, she just listened to me talk about it. And even though I tip-toed around with how those logistics might work, the discussion helped me to realize that I would have self-love issues to experience here by myself and that alone was enough to make me realize that I still had a purpose here.

So the process began of me taking care of Barbara. I was her caretaker and I administered the medicine to her. I lost all track of time and was completely absorbed in taking care of Barbara and making her as comfortable as possible at all times. She went from staying in our bed to a hospital bed in our bedroom.

As Barbara began to weaken, I saw that she was not really able to hold her body up and asked her to not try to walk by herself. Right after that she tried to go to the bathroom by herself when I was out of the room. When I returned I saw her putting her feet on the floor and I ran to help her but was too late and she fell to the floor. She didn't acutely hurt herself, although the fall was uncomfortable.

When I went to pick her up I realized that she was no longer able to control her body. I was able to get her upright and we walked a few feet and we both fell to the floor. I was not strong enough to hold her up by myself with her not being able to give me any help at all. Our bodies were entangled as we lay on the floor. True to form, even in her condition, Barbara could still use her mind and she was trying to figure out how to untangle us in such a way that we could then get her to the bathroom without falling down again.

I thought about that and how mentally strong she was as we lay there trying to get us untangled and her to the bathroom. I told her to just lay still and rest and I'd figure it out. I closed my eyes and said, "Holy Spirit, I know there is a solution to this, that we are not going to have to lay here indefinitely. It is all yours." As soon as I thought the word "yours" the doorbell rang. I told Barbara our prayers had been answered and I jumped up to see what angel spirit had sent to help us.

It was the social worker from hospice whom I had met once. She was on her way home and decided to stop for an impromptu visit. I quickly summarized our situation as we ran back to the bedroom together and got Barbara to the bathroom and then put her back in bed. The social worker said that Barbara needed a hospital bed and bedside toilet and I agreed to it. She made the call and it was delivered almost immediately even though we lived way out in a remote rural community.

Barbara's time in that small hospital bed was a couple of weeks at most. She slowly went from being able to talk to me to only being able to make a few sounds and then finally no sound at all.

The Last Popsicle

The hospital bed was perpendicular to our bed in the bedroom. On the first morning Barbara was in the hospital bed I brought my laptop into the bedroom to do the online teaching that I was doing for a university. She saw me walk in and said, "Sit over there so I can see you," and pointed to the right side of the hospital bed, the way she was facing. I was going to sit there anyway, but that touched me so much because I realized that about all she had left in this world was an occasional view of me sitting beside her bed.

Just as the hospice manager had said, Barbara got to the point where she wasn't eating anymore. The manager had told me that Barbara's body would be dehydrating and that giving her liquids would help her feel better.

During this period Barbara told me she would like to have fruit popsicles so that's what I gave her. In fact, part of the last Popsicle I gave her is still in the popsicle box in the freezer with a napkin wrapped around the stick part of it. Although I've long since given away all of her clothes and cleaned out all of the things like that, I can't seem to throw that box of popsicles away. It is just so very, very personal, so very, very Barbara. I didn't even think about it the first many months after she was gone but I noticed it a while back and realized that I'm keeping it without even realizing I've been keeping it. I know that I'll throw it away when I'm ready to throw it away.

Anyway, right toward the very end, Barbara couldn't really talk anymore and early one morning, around 1:30 or so, when I was up with her, she was making some sounds and trying to talk. I was listening intently for what she wanted when finally she said, very, very slowly, the word, "gewürztraminer". For those of you that know wine, you know that gewürztraminer is a sweet type of white wine and it is one of the types of wine that Barbara and I never, ever drank. I said, "Barbara, you don't even like gewürztraminer." Then it came to me and I said, "Oh, do you want a popsicle?" And she nodded her head yes. I ran to the freezer out in the garage and was so happy that I figured out what she wanted. Obviously, in her state of slowly beginning to leave the body, with her mind disengaging, the sweetness of gewürztraminer must have related in her mind to the sweetness of a popsicle and that's how she was able to communicate to me that she wanted a popsicle.

Pure Love Personified

One of Barbara's traits, that only my sister Phyllis knows, until now, is that she would often sort of go into a childlike mode. She would simply sound and act childlike and it was one of the things that I liked, and admired, most about Barbara. I saw that as her having access to all parts of her, including the childlikeness of childhood even as an adult.

To me, for most adults, and all adults I've ever known, our childlikeness has long since been covered over by our conditioning and, because of that, I was just amazed, and delighted, that Barbara could still access her childlikeness. In that moment when she said in her little baby voice, "ge-wurz-tra-mi-ner", I felt like I was seeing and hearing the most precious thing I had ever heard. The innocence and purity of Barbara in that moment somehow opened my heart even more than it was already opened and all I could do was cry tears of innocent oneness of being in that moment with her. I've only told one or two people about that experience because it is so sacred to me. But now I'm telling the world because I believe it is something worth sharing with you. A holy relationship embodies the innocence of each other in that relationship. It is pure love personified.

You Finally Balanced It

Barbara left the body on August 31, 2010. At 8:30 that morning I was sitting on the right side of her bed and closed my eyes to meditate. I immediately saw the spirit of Barbara floating in a standing position just above her body and facing me. She was glowing with love and power as she said to me, "You finally balanced it, (she used her favorite nickname for me)". I told her "Thank you, (I used my favorite nickname for her)" and felt as close to her as I ever have. All of our life together I had been working so hard to get my mind off of myself and onto her. I knew she was telling me that I had finally quit being self-focused and had given her all of myself. It is perhaps the best feeling I have ever had in my life.

I sat by the side of Barbara's bed all day that day. Around 4 P.M. I got up to go get something in the kitchen. As I began to move, she made a murmuring sound. I knew that she didn't want me to leave. I told her that I would be right back, which I was. I returned and continued holding her hands in mine like I had done all day. She was doing the ultra-slow breathing that the hospice manager told me she would do, with extremely long inhalations, extremely long pauses in between and extremely long exhalations.

I closed my eyes to be able to commune with her better and then I realized that the next day was September 1, our 21st wedding anniversary. When I realized that, I said (non-verbally, in a silent communication to her), "Oh! You're waiting until tomorrow to go. You don't have to do that, (I called her by my favorite nickname for her). You can go now."

With that I opened my eyes and saw her take a deep inhalation. Then I waited but knew she would not be exhaling. And she didn't. She had taken her last breath and had left the body.

I said out loud to her, "You're gone aren't you?" I felt

hollow inside, and numb. I looked over my left shoulder at the electric clock beside our bed that I kept synched with my cell phone. I wanted to see what time she had left the body because of my interest in numerology, not as anything causal, but as a reflection of her intention. It was 4:40 P.M.

Barbara and I loved what we called "mastery" numbers, which in numerology are all double numbers. And we also knew that anytime a mastery number has a zero with it, that it has a lot of power behind it. Barbara left the planet on the quadruple mastery number, 44, with a zero behind it, indicating unlimited power. When I saw that I smiled inwardly, even though I felt hollow inside, because I knew that Barbara left at 4:40 as a way of letting me know that was her intention and that she was back fully in her power.

I can't speak for Barbara now, but if she were still in the physical I know she would agree with me that we were two of the happiest people ever to be in a committed couple relationship. What we had was certainty and, in this life, that's saying a lot.

For me, my relationship with Barbara was the most amazing experience of my life, from the beginning to the end. She and I truly were not just married, but were also life partners, playmates, pathmates, lovers and best friends. Our love was certain. There was no doubt. And we trusted each other completely. And, in the end, we found ourselves in each other.

Epilogue

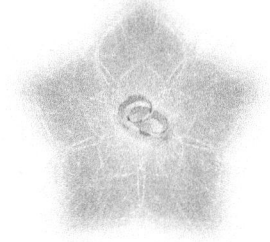

He has seen someone else as himself.[24]
—A Course in Miracles

When the gentle man from the funeral home put Barbara's body in a black bag in our bedroom, it didn't startle me. I knew she was not in that body anymore. At the funeral of her father years before, Barbara told me she knew, as soon as she saw her father's body in the coffin, that he was not in that body. And she said that helped her move forward on her spiritual path. But as Barbara's body was slowly put into the back of a hearse, I began to feel more hollow. As the door to the hearse closed, I began to feel estranged from Barbara. And as the hearse slowly drove away out of what used to be "our" driveway, I felt the finality of Barbara being gone from the physical and I slowly backed away to the farthest corner of the driveway and broke down into tears like I had never cried before. My mourning had begun.

The next day I gathered up all the materials from our home that I wanted to use to plan Barbara's funeral. I was to be the minister, so to speak, or the facilitator, of Barbara's funeral. The day after that I was on a plane to Houston and that is when I planned the funeral. I had an aisle seat, which was amazing considering that I booked the flight the day before departure. And all the way to Houston I listened to the meditative, ambient music that Barbara and I had played driving back and forth to the hospital during her two sick periods of being in the hospital. This was the same music I played for Barbara during her last five weeks until, one day, she asked me to turn it off and I never turned it on again until on that flight. With earphones on, my eyes closed and a legal pad in my lap, I literally cried during the whole plane ride as I planned the funeral using Barbara's own journals as the essence of what I wanted to share at the funeral.

It was very strange seeing Barbara's picture on a television monitor as I walked into the funeral home. I was the first to arrive, with my mother and step-father. Slowly the large room began to fill with people, all of whom I knew, until it was filled to capacity.

On the written funeral program that I had designed

with Barbara's dear friend, Amy, was the inscription, "Prayers and affirmations from Barbara". I began and ended the funeral with the most intimate of ideas from Barbara about her relationship with God. There was not a dry eye in the room. The room was filled with people whose lives had been touched and changed by Barbara and I invited anyone that wanted to share ideas about Barbara to speak and many did.

The resultant milieu was a combination of pure love, heartbreak and loving remembrances of their dear friend, Barbara. I concluded with words from Barbara and, on the last word, I felt the life come out of my body as I slowly crumpled to the floor. As I was feeling my energy leave my body, my heart leapt as I thought, "Oh, I *am* going to have a heart attack and leave the body now", which I had thought about before. And I was overjoyed at that. But as my younger brother, Ferdie, rushed to my side I realized that I wasn't leaving the body and that I was just letting go of the energy that I had used to be able to get through the process that began at 4:40 on August 31 and had just ended.

I regained my composure and the funeral director asked me if I wanted him to remove the three rings on Barbara's fingers. I said, "No, thank you. I'll do it myself". There was our wedding ring and two other rings that Barbara dearly loved. One represented the power of God to Barbara and the other represented His love of her. And they both had diamonds in them to represent her eternal relationship with God.

After spending several days with my Mom and my step-father, two very loving and supportive souls, in the town where I was born and raised in Louisiana, I was back in "our" home in California. Even though it was very strange being alone in our home, as Barbara would say it, the house "hugged me" and it felt good to be there.

Breakfastation

I cried myself to sleep that first night. In the morning I began what I called a "breakfastation" to myself, meaning a combination of breakfast and meditation. I would start with reading from Barbara's journals, until I had reread all of them.

Days or weeks later I would begin by reading one or more "readings" from our guides, all of which I had previously transcribed directly onto paper as they were being given to me by a guide, or other loving entity, through Barbara as channel. I learned how to take notes very fast when I was a freshman at L.S.U. and have never lost that talent.

At the same time, after reading Barbara's ideas, or ideas from our guides, I would read *A Course in Miracles*. I started with the ten characteristics of God's teachers in the *Manual for Teachers* because I knew I would get solace and strength from that part of the course and it helped me tremendously.

I read one characteristic each day and would then close my eyes and meditate, or reflect, on that characteristic and would commune with spirit about it and how to apply it to myself and out in the world. When I finished with those ten characteristics I studied the whole *Manual for Teachers* in the same manner. And then I started rereading, or studying, the *Text* once again.

I had just finished rereading the *Text* shortly before Barbara's last bout of sickness, those last five weeks. I always read *A Course in Miracles* very slowly, very deliberately in a meditative way for maximal learning and application. And I always meditate and reflect on what I've read to help me absorb, take in, and integrate what I'm reading. This time I made up my mind that I was not going to go on to the next thing, whether it was a word, idea or sentence, until I knew that I understood what it was saying to me.

My breakfastations took a long time each day. But I never looked at a clock, I never concerned myself about time, for two reasons. And I still do that to this day. I knew that time was a construct made up by the ego and I knew that it was easy enough to fall into an unconscious egoic state so I didn't want to intentionally activate my ego by focusing on time. The other reason is that I intentionally wanted my breakfastations to be the most important thing in my life and I therefore didn't want to limit them with some made up time limit or even to measure them by how long they took. I don't know how long my breakfastations took, but by the time I finished and was moving around the house enough to inadvertently see what time it was, my best guess was somewhere between two and four hours.

I knew that my breakfastations were going to be about my mourning Barbara's leaving the physical, my healing through the mourning, and for what I still refer to in meditation as "I want to live the purpose for which I am still here".

Barbara's Presence

From the very moment that I got home after the funeral, I began to feel Barbara's presence. It was easy for me and still is. What I would experience were bouts of deep sorrow, of feeling lost without Barbara, fear of being alone and fear of life. However, I also had a very clear sense, and understanding, that I was now physically alone in the world and that was not going to change. My acceptance of that was immediate. It came from the years of Barbara's and my study and training that there really is no past and there really is no future. Everything is right here, right now. And I knew it was up to me to decide how to live. I could be a victim of Barbara's leaving the physical and make up things in my mind about the past and the future that would cause me to not be present in the here and now. Or I could be at cause for how I would live in each moment. I chose the latter approach to life.

Every morning, then, for a very long time, I would experience a combination of deep sorrow and then ultimate resolution, acceptance and a sense of being fully engaged in life. As I would delve deeply into Barbara's journals, for example, all of a sudden sadness would change into sorrow and ultimately into the deepest despondency that I've ever known. Twice in this despondent state I somehow fell out of my chair at the dining table and onto the floor. I would be crying my eyes out and feeling completely hollow and despondent and then just collapse into a heap just like I did at Barbara's funeral.

The Power of Love

During those early weeks after Barbara's funeral, I would daily reach some kind of an emotional peak of despair and, consciously, I would allow it fully, willingly, so that I could feel the fullness of the emotional pain. And every time, with no exception, the pain would eventually begin to dissipate as I would feel myself opening up inside. It was like a crescendo of emotional pain and then all of a sudden I would feel like I was cracking open until ultimately I felt like I had cracked wide open. And as I seemed to crack open, which is exactly how it felt, there was also a profound sense of stillness within me. Then I would always feel a palpable transformation from the depths of despair into what I began to call the power of love.

I had applied this approach to emotional pain to myself for years, and taught it to clients, but I had never felt its transformative powers to this extent until I went through my own version of the healing process of mourning the "loss" of Barbara. Ever since then, either in the moment of pain, or after the experience of some kind of emotional pain followed by getting still and feeling the pain fully, I have always had the experience of releasing the emotional pain and discovering the underlying false belief about myself that was stimulated in me by either someone or something.

Along with that, I have also always found the power of love underneath the pain. I now don't believe that you have to experience the "death" of someone in order to use this process. I think what is absolutely necessary, however, is the complete willingness and total desire to feel the pain fully.

Integrated Within Me

Ever since Barbara left the physical, I have felt her integrated within me. And for many, many months I would commune with Barbara on a regular, daily basis. She was the first thing on my mind in the morning and the last thing at night. But it was not in the form of memories or in lamenting what might have been in the future. It was always in the present moment.

We were always connected and if I would be still, fully present in the moment, I would feel a communion with her. To this day, if a memory of her pops in my mind, or is stimulated by some physical circumstance, or someone, I let it go instantly because I know that life does not exist in the past. I know this may sound cold and aloof to some of you, but I know, without a shadow of a doubt, that Barbara would not be living in the past either if I had left the physical instead of her.

Barbara never lived in the past while she was here. I was the one that did that. Now, because of my life experiences with Barbara, especially the last five weeks and the intense mourning, I have learned how to live fully present in the moment. It's very easy for me to do when I'm alone. The challenges are when I am out in the world. And that's why I am still here. Now, because of Barbara, I see the world differently and am able to appreciate my oneness with everyone and everything.

Does it Serve Love?

One day I came home from being out in the world. I sat down and closed my eyes to meditate about Barbara. What came to me immediately was that I was still relying on Barbara as a crutch to make my way through the world. There is nothing "wrong" with crutches. Jesus told us that once when he and Barbara were communicating. It is better to have a crutch and therefore not induce additional fear within you than to not have a crutch and induce more fear. But I wanted to know, in the language Barbara and I used, "Does it serve me?" Even better, "Does it serve love?" And "Does it serve the purpose for which I am still here?"

While I was taking care of Barbara during those last five weeks of her life I never, not one time, thought about my future without her. And on the first day back home after the funeral, I knew, deep inside of me, that I was still here so that I could learn how to take care of myself in this world by allowing the power of love to flow through me and extend it out into the world. Those last five weeks of taking care of Barbara had polished off some single digit percentage of responsibility that I had still been giving to her in minor, subtle ways.

In this short but poignant meditation, I became aware that I was still giving Barbara responsibility for my life in a psychic way. In communing with her as Barbara, I had been seeing her as separate from me and was relying on what I thought she had that I didn't have. And I knew that was violating the purpose for which I was still here. So I made the decision, right then and there, that it didn't serve me to continue to actively commune with Barbara. I knew she was integrated within me and now it was time for me to live, to experience, that integration in order to make it real for me.

The Last Goodbye

I communed with Barbara deeply about this and knew that she understood and agreed with my decision. I then told her goodbye one more time while acknowledging our oneness. Now I just "know" my oneness with Barbara. I just don't actively communicate with her.

Barbara was literally my savior, not figuratively or virtually; she was *literally* my savior. She told me that she was going to fix my broken wings so that I could fly again, and she did. She saw in me her own interests. And she taught me how to see in her my own. My dreams were her dreams, her dreams were my dreams and all of our dreams were our dreams.

Barbara's Epitaph

This epilogue is the same as Barbara's epitaph: we are as God created us and there is only one we. Paradoxically, we see ourselves at the mercy of the world, its inhabitants and the laws of the universe. The ultimate sad thing is that we believe God created the physical universe, the universe of form, and if we are "good" and "right" we'll get to Heaven.

Barbara knew that we are already in Heaven but have dreamed up a hell on Earth to "protect" us from the responsibility of living in the love and power that is our essence and, in so doing, extending creation just as God extended it to us.

The message of our holy relationship, from Barbara and I to each of you, is to accept the love that you are and see it in everyone and everything, not in the form in how it appears, but in its essence. In so doing, your life will be a holy relationship with the world and everyone and everything in it.

Appendix

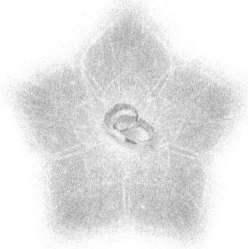

This book is not about *A Course in Miracles*. However, the course is embedded within the spirit of this book and I have quoted from it liberally. In 1986 I was inside of what could best be called a New Age bookstore in Baton Rouge for the purpose of evaluating the potential sale of a small shopping center that the bookstore was a part of. As I was waiting for the owner of the shopping center, who also owned the bookstore, I browsed through the bookstore.

I had been on a spiritual path since September of 1980 but I had never been to a full-fledged New Age bookstore. Titles of all kinds seemed to spring off the shelves and into my mind in a way that the whole bookstore began to resonate inside of me in the most beneficial of ways. I was mesmerized by the bookstore and highly attracted to it.

As I turned the corner of one of the aisles I bumped into a small stack of blue books on the floor that were still partially wrapped in cellophane. I could see that the title of the books was *A Course in Miracles*. My mind reeled when I saw the title. I was terrified and exuberant all at the same time. Was this book about how to perform miracles?

I so wanted to pick one up but I was afraid and embarrassed. It seemed like if I picked one up I would be exposing myself to whoever might see me (no one was in the store) as a fanatic for even considering looking at, much less buying, the book.

The owner came down from his office shortly thereafter and that put me out of my misery and the book out of my mind. But shortly thereafter I was in a study group at the local Unity church and someone mentioned *A Course in Miracles*. I commented that I had just seen the book at that bookstore. From there the conversation led me to believe that the book was worthy of my consideration and it was not long after that I purchased the book.

That book, my original copy of *A Course in Miracles*, is like an old friend to me now. I have wondered dozens of times in whose hands it will end up when I leave the physical because it has given me so much love and my own love energy is now so infused within the pages of that book. I now know that it holds the original copyright of *A Course in Miracles*, which is 1975. It also has the next updated copyright of the course, which is 1985.

Most students of the course now use the 1992 second edition. It has some editing revisions and therefore the page numbers are different from the first edition. I have been pondering for a long time whether I need to get the second edition and convert all of my quotation references that I've used in writing *A Holy Relationship* to the second edition page numbers.

However, I have decided to use my original edition references for the following reasons. Barbara and I both used the original edition. I still have her copy and use it as a book rest to lean my copy on every morning when I read and meditate from the course. So the original edition is very personal to me, as is *A Holy Relationship*. Also, this is not a book *about A Course in Miracles*. I have a couple of those in mind, and before I write them I will get the second, or most current, edition of the course and use that as my reference source.

I was also taught in graduate school to reference whatever source I use in any writing that I do. I've actually used my own copy of the course, the original edition, so that would mean that I would reference, or cite, the original edition as my reference. However, I would be going against the trend of what most all authors now seem to be doing, which is to not only use and reference the second edition, but to also use a detailed iconography to lead the reader not only to the exact page, but from the exact chapter, section of the chapter and paragraph of the section to the exact line containing the quotation.

Because of knowing all of this about book references, and the course references in particular, I was concerned about using my original copy of the course as the reference source. So I was tempted to get the second edition and find all the references that I've used in the second edition and list those as my references.

But these days I don't make any decisions unless it feels like an intuitive knowing from deep within. So I reflected deeply about this in meditation and what I got was that the ideas that I have drawn into this book from *A Course in Miracles* are complete unto themselves within *A Holy Relationship*. They need no further study in order to be understood within the context of this book.

And, if further study is warranted by any reader of the second edition of the course, then that reader will be lead to that part of the second edition for further study. This may be a fancy way of me avoiding doing the extra work of converting to the second edition of the course, but my heart is in the first edition, and the first edition is in this book, so that is what I am offering to the reader and why. I hope you can appreciate my reasoning and my method of making the decision.

I also want to point out that I don't have the page numbers listed in the References section of this book for two quotes from the Swiss psychiatrist, Carl Jung. I found the quotes in Barbara's graduate school thesis in a special section of her thesis called, Inspiration, which is just before the actual thesis, or the presentation of her research and research findings. I was able to determine, from my own research, which books these two quotes came from, which were also listed in the References section of Barbara's thesis and are now listed in the References section of this book.

References

1. Foundation for Inner Peace (1985). *A course in miracles* (text, p. 132). Tiburon, CA.
2. Ibid (p. 404).
3. Foundation for Inner Peace (1985). *A course in miracles* (workbook for students, p. 245). Tiburon, CA.
4. Barks, C. (2004). *The essential Rumi* (p. 106). New York, NY: HarperOne.
5. Bartholomew (1986). *I come as a brother: A remembrance of illusions* (p. 171). Taos, N.M.: High Mesa Press.
6. Foundation for Inner Peace (1985). *A course in miracles* (Text, p. 16). Tiburon, CA.
7. Ibid (p. 407).
8. Shakespeare. *The tempest*, Act 5, Scene 1.
9. Jung, C. G. (1959). *The collected works of C. G. Jung: AION researches into the phenomenology of the self*, vol. 9, 2nd ed., Bollingen series xx. Princeton, NJ: Princeton University Press.

10. Foundation for Inner Peace (1985). *A course in miracles* (manual for teachers, p. 5). Tiburon, CA.

11. Foundation for Inner Peace (1985). *A course in miracles* (workbook for students, p. 311). Tiburon, CA.

12. Foundation for Inner Peace (1985). *A course in miracles* (manual for teachers, p. 27). Tiburon, CA.

13. Foundation for Inner Peace (1985). *A course in miracles* (text, p. 18). Tiburon, CA.

14. Foundation for Inner Peace (1985). *A course in miracles* (workbook for students, p. 280). Tiburon, CA.

15. Foundation for Inner Peace (1985). *A course in miracles* (text, p. 202). Tiburon, CA.

16. Ibid (p. 289).

17. Ibid (p. 299).

18. Jung, C. G. (1966). *The collected works of C. G. Jung: The practice of psychotherapy*, vol. 16, 2nd. ed., Bollingen series xx. Princeton, NJ: Princeton University Press.

19. Foundation for Inner Peace (1985). *A course in miracles.* (manual for teachers, p. 5). Tiburon, CA.

20. Jung, C. G. (1966). *The collected works of C. G. Jung: The practice of psychotherapy*, vol. 16, 2nd. ed., Bollingen series xx. Princeton, NJ: Princeton University Press.

21. Foundation for Inner Peace (1985). *A course in miracles* (workbook for students, pp. 246-247). Tiburon, CA.

22. Foundation for Inner Peace (1985). *A course in miracles* (text, p. 300). Tiburon, CA.

23. Rodegast, P. & Stanton, J. (1985). *Immanuel's book* (p. 203). New York: Bantam Books.

24. Foundation for Inner Peace (1985). *A course in miracles* (manual for teachers, p. 3). Tiburon, CA.

About the Author

Jimmie Lewis is a licensed psychotherapist with a Master of Arts degree in Counseling Psychology with a double major in transpersonal psychology and couple counseling. With his deceased wife, Barbara, they did thesis research on their own relationship with each as co-researcher for the other's thesis. They used this work and their co-spiritual path as the basis for their own relationship and the counseling work they did with couples.

Barbara and Jimmie are co-authors of two books. *The Energy of Life* is a primer on how the world works and how we create the lives that we experience. *The Real Miracle* is a real life example of how to find peace in this world of challenges by knowing and applying who and what we really are.

As an entrepreneur with an M.B.A. from Tulane University, Jimmie has always been a teacher in one form or another and his work has always been to help people discover their inner power by knowing their inner essence. He sees all of life as spiritual and applies a psychospiritual approach to everything he does.

Jimmie has been on a spiritual path since 1980 and a practitioner of *A Course in Miracles* since 1986.

Jimmie's talent is in helping people to transform fear into the power of love.

He works with individuals and couples, and groups focused on a single vision, to help them create the life they want.

And he facilitates *A Course in Miracles* study groups and conducts experiential workshops to facilitate awakening to the truths inherent in the course.

For personal appearances, workshops, retreats, group or private sessions:

jimmie@jimmielewis.com
www.jimmielewis.com

www.ingramcontent.com/pod-product-compliance
Lightning Source LLC
Chambersburg PA
CBHW071908290426
44110CB00013B/1327